Raspberry Pi For Kids®

FOR

DUMMIES®
A Wiley Brand

by Richard Wentk

FOR
DUMMIES®
A Wiley Brand

Raspberry Pi For Kids For Dummies®

Published by: **John Wiley & Sons, Inc.,** 111 River Street, Hoboken, NJ 07030-5774, www.wiley.com

Copyright © 2015 by John Wiley & Sons, Inc., Hoboken, New Jersey

Published simultaneously in Canada

For general information on our other products and services, please contact our Customer Care Department within the U.S. at 877-762-2974, outside the U.S. at 317-572-3993, or fax 317-572-4002. For technical support, please visit www.wiley.com/techsupport.

Wiley publishes in a variety of print and electronic formats and by print-on-demand. Some material included with standard print versions of this book may not be included in e-books or in print-on-demand. If this book refers to media such as a CD or DVD that is not included in the version you purchased, you may download this material at http://booksupport.wiley.com. For more information about Wiley products, visit www.wiley.com.

Library of Congress Control Number: 2015941231

ISBN 978-1-119-04951-7 (pbk); ISBN 978-1-119-04982-1 (ePDF); ISBN 978-1-119-04949-4 (ePub)

Manufactured in the United States of America

10 9 8 7 6 5 4 3 2 1

Contents at a Glance

Table of Contents

Introduction

How much do you know about computers? Most people can play games, watch videos, listen to music, and explore the Internet without knowing much at all. The computer just works, and that's all they care about.

Do you want to know more? What really happens when you click a mouse, press a key on a keyboard, click a link on a website, or launch an app?

And more — how do you make a website? How do you make an app? Or a game?

Are these interesting questions? If not, that's totally fine. Not everyone gets excited about making things.

But if you do, here's a bigger question: How can you find the answers? A book like this one can help you get started, but figuring out how to find your own answers will get you further than reading someone else's ideas.

Understanding computers teaches you that it's good to be able to solve puzzles, understand math, write code, and build things that are clever and useful. But it's even better for helping you to know that *you can learn* how to do all these things.

Even if you don't really care about code, you can use coding as a way to check how good you are at learning something new.

Being able to find answers is more than half the problem. After you've researched a problem, you can add something of your own to the work everyone else has done. Sharing what you make helps everyone else, too.

Don't think of this book as a set of school problems. It's not about passing or failing. A lot of the projects are suggestions and ideas to get you started. They're not so much like step-by-step guides you can follow without understanding what's happening. For some of them, you need to break out of the book and find your own answers online.

Some of the projects are hard. If they're too hard for you, it's fine to think of simpler projects of your own and maybe come back to the hard projects later.

Or not. It doesn't matter as long as *you* are having fun and doing stuff you think is cool. Especially if you surprise yourself with what you can do.

So don't give up when you find something hard or decide you're stupid and should be doing something else. Here's a big secret: Everyone who writes code feels like that at least some of the time. No exceptions.

And here's another big secret: When you discover you can do something amazing, it's totally worth it.

About This Book

Raspberry Pi For Kids For Dummies introduces you to the world of the tiny Raspberry Pi computer.

Some people will tell you the Raspberry Pi was designed for kids and is easy to use. This isn't untrue, but it's not totally true, either. In some ways, the Pi is very easy to use. In others, it can be harder than a Mac or a PC.

But the Pi is really good for learning how computers work on the inside and for building simple software and hardware projects. It's also good for learning more about learning, which means finding out how to do your own research on the Internet.

With this book as your guide, you will discover

✔ What a Raspberry Pi is

✔ How the different versions of the Pi have changed over time

✔ What extra parts you need and how much they cost

✔ Where to find the extra parts if you don't already have them

✔ How to connect them to your Pi

✔ What to do to download and install the latest software for a Pi

✔ How to power up a Pi

✔ Everything about working with the most important settings

✔ Why you need to power down a Pi safely

✔ The ins and outs of the Linux operating system

✔ How to use the Pi's Linux desktop

✔ How to find files using the desktop File Manager

✔ What the different Linux directories do

✔ The difference between an ordinary user and the Linux god-user

✔ How to type Linux commands from the keyboard

✔ What you can do with Scratch, a simple programming system

✔ How to start creating a simple game in Scratch

✔ Why the Sonic Pi music programming system is a ton of fun

✔ How you can create art with a program called TuxPaint

- How to write code and draw pictures using the popular Python language

- How to make your own web server

- More about making your web server smarter

- How you can use Python to control your character in the Pi version of Minecraft

- How to make a simple webcam

- Which parts and extras you need to start making hardware projects

- How to build a simple thermometer

- How to make a web page for a hardware project

Foolish Assumptions

Raspberry Pi For Kids For Dummies makes some guesses about what you do and don't know already. You don't need to know anything about code or about how computers work on the inside. This book does assume the following:

- You can use a Mac or a PC or maybe even a Linux computer.

- You're comfortable with a mouse and keyboard, and you can find your way around your computer's desktop.

- You're not scared of plugging together computer parts to add extras.

- You're fine with using Google or some other search engine to find things on the Internet.

- You have a little (but not much) cash to spare. Fifty dollars will cover most of what you need, and $100 will cover everything easily.

Icons Used in This Book

Throughout the margins of this book are little round pictures known as icons. Here's what those icons signify:

The text next to this icon offers tips for completing tasks or for making your job easier. You'll want to take advantage of these nuggets of wisdom!

Pay special attention when you see this icon. It points out information you'll want to make sure to remember.

This text warns you of things that can go wrong . . . very wrong!

This icon marks text that tells you all the technical details you may or may not be interested in. If you don't care, you can skip this text without missing anything.

Beyond This Book

The fun doesn't stop with this book. Online, you will find the following goodies:

- ✔ **Cheat Sheet:** You can find this book's Cheat Sheet online at www.dummies.com/cheatsheet/raspberrypiforkids. See the Cheat Sheet for checklists.

- ✔ **Dummies.com online articles and chapters:** You can find companion articles and bonus chapters for this book online at www.dummies.com/extras/raspberrypiforkids.

- ✔ **Updates:** If this book has any updates after printing, they'll be posted to www.dummies.com/updates/raspberrypiforkids.

Where to Go from Here

Like other *For Dummies* books, *Raspberry Pi For Kids For Dummies* is a reference. That means you can read it in the order that makes sense to you. You can flip through it to find new ideas, or you can use the table of contents and index to zero in on exactly the topic you're looking for.

You also have the option to read this book like a book, from beginning to end. If you're a complete beginner, I recommend you work through at least the first few chapters in order. If you're new to the Raspberry Pi, those early chapters have everything you need to get started.

Some later chapters assume that you've worked your way through earlier chapters or you already know the topics they cover. The last few chapters are projects that tie together a lot of earlier details. It's best not to jump into them unless you already know some of the basics!

Good luck — and don't forget to have fun and do cool things!

Week 1
Making a Pi

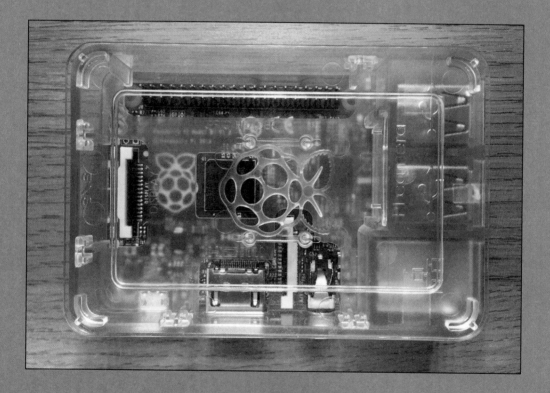

In this part, you'll . . .

Visit http://www.dummies.com for great
Dummies content online.

Find Parts for Your Pi

The Raspberry Pi is a super-cool, super-small, super-cheap microcomputer. In fact, it's a super-cool, super-small, super-cheap microcomputer *board,* and it doesn't do much on its own. Before you can do super-clever things with it, you have to add some extras to build a Pi system.

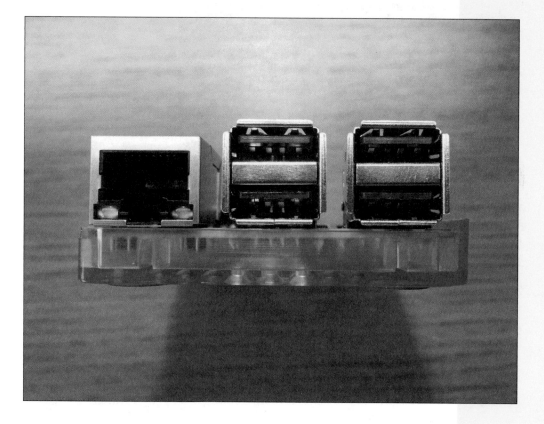

Understand the Pi

The Raspberry Pi, shown in Figure 1-1, is a tiny computer developed in the UK by the Raspberry Pi Foundation (www. raspberrypi.org). It's much smaller than a Mac or PC — it's almost exactly the same size as a credit card! And it's also much cheaper. (Prices vary, but a Pi costs around $30 in the United States and between £20 to £30 in the UK.)

Figure 1-1

The Pi only comes in Raspberry. There is no Apple Pi, Blueberry Pi, or Pumpkin Pi. A lot of people like Raspberry, so that's fine with Pi fans.

Here are a few of the things you can do with a Pi:

- Learn how computers work

- Make and play games

- Learn how to program

- Make web pages

- Make digital music

- Build simple electronic projects

✔ Design awesome Minecraft worlds

✔ Have a ton of fun!

What you can't do with a Pi

Although the Pi is a fully working computer, it's not a Mac, a PC, a tablet, or a games console. It's not as powerful as more expensive computers. Here are some things you can't do with a Pi:

✔ Run Microsoft Windows, or any Windows software

✔ Download and play apps or games from the Apple App Store

✔ Develop software for Windows, iOS, or OS X

✔ Use popular web browsers like Chrome, Safari, IE, or Firefox

✔ Play popular mainstream commercial games

Does that seem disappointing? It shouldn't.

What you can do with a Pi that you can't do with a bigger computer

To make up for it, you can do a lot of things with a Pi you can't do with a bigger computer. For example, you can

✔ Wipe your Pi in minutes and start from scratch if you make a bad mistake

✔ Experiment with writing your own software

✔ Build projects that do useful things and save money

✔ Rewrite and customize all the software in your Pi

✔ Make your Pi do something at certain times of day, or on dates you choose, or when a sensor notices a change

The Pi story explained

The Pi follows an old British tradition. Back in the 1980s, the UK led the world in computers and computer companies with fancy names, like the Spectrum, the Dragon, the Tangerine, and the Acorn. These computers were much less powerful than the Pi, but many kids learned how to program on them. Some of those kids became professional software developers, and one of them went on to develop the Pi.

The Raspberry Pi Foundation wants to help the kids of the 2010s follow the same route and to have fun along the way.

✔ Connect thermometers, cameras, motion sensors, and other extras

✔ Leave Pi projects running 24/7 without using a lot of electricity

You can see now why the Pi is special. Unlike a PC or a Mac, it's so small and cheap you can buy a separate Pi for every project. You can leave it running all the time. And it comes with a good set of simple tools for writing software — all free.

Discover the Different Pi Models

Pi boards come in different types (see Table 1-1). You need to know about the differences so that you don't buy the wrong one.

The older models are called the A and B boards. The newer models are called the A+ and B+ boards. As of early 2015, there's an even newer, faster, shinier, and better board called the Pi 2.

Figure 1-2 shows a Model B+ and a Model B.

The boards are the same size, and they use the same software. But they have different numbers of connectors and other bits and pieces.

Figure 1-2

I'll make it easy to choose: You want a Pi 2. The older models are out of date now. You can still buy them, but the Pi 2 is much better for almost everything.

What's the deal with the A+? It's a cut-down budget Pi board with some important bits missing. It's definitely not the Pi you want when you're starting out.

It may, sometimes, kind of, perhaps be the right board for small finished projects. But don't get one until you've read the rest of this book!

Table 1-1	Comparing Raspberry Pi Models
Model	**What It's Good For**
A	Out of date now. Don't buy one!
B	Out of date.
A+	Smaller, cheaper, slower than a Pi 2. Only useful for special projects.
B+	Out of date. Get a Pi 2!
Pi 2 Model B	You want this one.

There is no Pi 2 Model A/A+ — at least, not yet. It's possible the Pi people will start selling one by the end of 2015. Or maybe 2016. Or never. You'll have to wait and see. If they do, it could be a cheaper option for finished projects. No one knows yet. And if it appears, your first Pi should still be a Pi 2 B, not an A.

Understand Pi Extras

When you buy a Raspberry Pi, you get a small circuit board. And that's it. On its own, the board does nothing. You can't do anything with it, except look at it, and maybe play catch, which is fun but not what it's made for.

Collect Pi parts

To turn a Pi board into a working computer, you have to add some extras. Collecting all the extras and connecting them to the Pi is your first project. And it's a big one!

Here's a list of what you need:

- USB hub with separate power (A and B models only)

- USB keyboard

✔ USB mouse

✔ Monitor or TV

✔ Memory card

✔ Power supply

✔ Long network cable

✔ Cables and connectors

 Try to do it yourself and ask for help from a grown-up only if you get stuck. You'll learn a lot about getting started with computers. If you want to save time and maybe money, skip to the "Collect Parts the Lazy Way" section, later in this chapter.

Decide whether you need a hub

Are you getting a Pi 2? You don't need a hub. Did you get an old Model A+ or B+ board? You don't need a hub either.

Otherwise, there's something you need to know: the original A/B models had a problem: If you plugged a keyboard and mouse into the USB connectors, the Pi often stopped working.

Figure 1-3 shows how you have to fix this issue by connecting everything to the Pi, including a keyboard, and mouse, through a USB hub.

 The hub has to have its own separate power supply. The hub solves the problem, but leaves you with a big mess of wires and connectors and stuff.

The A+/B+/2 models work fine without a hub, as shown in Figure 1-4. This makes them easier to set up. They don't need so many wires and cables.

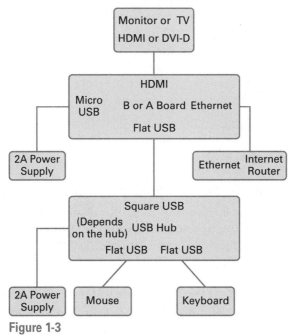

Figure 1-3

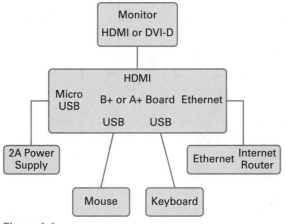

Figure 1-4

A *hub* is a box with plenty of USB connectors. You plug one end into a single socket on the Pi, and then you plug all your other USB extras into the hub. If the hub has its own power supply, it makes sure that everything gets the power it needs.

If you plug things that use a lot of electricity to whirr or flash, like robot motors and killer lasers, you need a hub even on a Model A/+ and B+. Small things like keyboards and mice don't need one.

Choose a mouse and keyboard

You can use any mouse or keyboard with a USB plug. Models with a cable should just work. You can *probably* use wireless models, as long as they come with a USB receiver dongle. (Anything made by Logitech should work.) Bluetooth mice and keyboards probably won't work.

You don't need to spend a lot of money on these extras. Basic models are fine.

You won't be using your Pi for serious gaming, so you don't need a Predator Ultra Galaxy Killer Destructo-Mouse with 15 buttons and a sharp and pointy design you can cut your fingers on. But if you have one spare, you can use it if you like. (The extra buttons won't do anything.)

Choose a monitor or TV

The Pi can work with a monitor or a TV.

The best way to connect the Pi to a monitor is to use the HDMI socket. Most new TVs and many monitors have an HDMI socket that takes an HDMI cable. Hook up the cable to the Pi at one end and the monitor or TV at other, and you're done.

Figure 1-5 shows where the HDMI connector is.

The monitor/TV doesn't have to be very new, or very good. The Pi can barely produce HD video. Almost any monitor less than ten years old should work fine.

Figure 1-5

A few monitors have a different socket called a DVI-D connector. If you can't find a monitor with HDMI, you need an *adaptor cable* with an HDMI plug at one end and a DVI plug at the other. Look on Amazon and eBay for a cheap one.

If your monitor has only a VGA connector, you need a special adaptor and a cable. Amazon and eBay should help again, but you may as well see whether you can find a used new or used monitor with the right connections. It may be cheaper than an adaptor.

 The Big Yellow Socket on the Model A/B Pis can work with an old-fashioned analog TV — the kind that lives in a huge wooden box with a heavy thick glass screen. Most people don't use them anymore. You shouldn't either because the picture will be very fuzzy, and you won't be able to read words on the screen.

 You don't really need a monitor at all because you can control a Pi remotely from another computer. This is called *running headless* — not because you can do it without your head, but because you don't need a monitor, mouse, or keyboard. (These are just like the Pi's head, kind of, if you use your imagination.) Setting up a headless Pi is kind of complicated, especially if you're just starting out. It works differently on a Mac and a PC. If you're curious, search the web for Headless Raspberry Pi. You probably won't be able to get it working until you've spent more time with your Pi.

Recognize cables and connectors

Wait — USB? VGA? DVI? HDMI? What do all these letters mean? If you don't already know, search the web to find out!

Type the letters into a browser search bar and see what you get. Search for images to see pictures.

You don't need to know how the cables work. You don't even need to remember that HDMI stands for High-Definition Multimedia Interface. (Like, really, who cares?)

But you do need to be able to tell cables apart so that you know which cable goes where on the Pi. You can also use the photos in this chapter as a guide. For example, Figure 1-6 shows the network/ Ethernet and USB connectors on the side of a B+ board.

Figure 1-6

Letter lists like these are called TLAs — Three-Letter Acronyms. To make an acronym, you take the first letter of every word in a complicated technical name and put it in order. This makes a shorter word that is easier to remember (but not always easier to say). There are a lot of TLAs in computing. Some of them have four letters, which doesn't make sense, but that's just how it is. You don't need to remember them all, but it helps to remember the ones that get used a lot.

Choose a memory card

The Pi doesn't have a disk drive. It stores everything on a small memory card. The Model A or B needs an SDHC card with a speed rating of 8 or 10. For a Model A+/ B+/2, get a microSD card.

Figure 1-7 shows the bottom of a Model B+. The memory card is the black rectangle at the right.

The card should hold at least 4GB. You can get a bigger card if you like, but it will cost more, and most of the space will be wasted.

Figure 1-7

 Some MicroSD cards come with an SDHC adaptor. If you get one of these you can use the same card in older A/B and newer A+/B+ Pi boards.

Find memory cards

The cheap option is to get a blank card — Amazon is a good choice — and write the software to the card by hand. You can only do this if your Mac or PC has a card reader/writer. If it doesn't, you'll have to buy one for about $5 to $10 (less than £10 in the UK).

The lazy option is to buy a card with the Pi software already installed. The software is called NOOBS. You can buy prewritten cards from Amazon and shops that specialize in Pi extras. The cards cost a few dollars or pounds more, but they save you some time.

Find a power supply

 Although the Pi is cheap to run, it needs a special power supply and a special cable. The power connector on the Pi is a tiny microUSB socket, and it needs a matching plug. The socket grips the power cable hard so that you can't pull it out by accident.

You can use a standard USB power supply as long as it's 2A, 2.1A, or 2100mA. This means it produces plenty of spare power. If it isn't labeled 2A, 2.1A, or 2100mA, your Pi may not work properly.

The best way to find a power supply is to look for Raspberry Pi Power Supply online. Don't forget to look for the 2A tag!

 Some cheaper supplies are labeled 1500mA or 1.5A. They'll probably work, until you start plugging in lots of extras. It's worth spending a little more and getting more power. Some Apple iPad adaptors produce 2.4A. That's even better than 2.1A. If you have one, you can use one.

Other cables

You'll probably need a network cable, which is sometimes called an *Ethernet cable.* The cable should be Cat 5 or Cat 6. Plug one end of the cable into your home Internet router and the other into the network socket on the Pi.

If you want to plug more than one Pi to a home network, buy a long cable and a *network switch* — a box with lots of network sockets. Plug the long cable into one of the sockets and other computers into the other sockets. The other end of the cable goes into your home router. (If this is too hard, ask a grown-up to help you. If you can't find a grown-up to help, search the web!)

 'Cat doesn't mean meow here. It's short for Category 5/6, which is a very boring description and means your cable is good and fast. Cat 4, 3, 2, 1 cables won't work.

Add Optional Extras

You can add a lot of extras to your Pi. You don't need them to get started, but they can give you more options and maybe make your Pi easier to use.

Choose a case

You don't really need a case, but a good one will help protect your Pi from falling objects, fat fingers, and annoying brothers or sisters.

Search the web for Raspberry Pi case to see a very long list of cases. Pick one that looks good. They all do more or less the same thing. A/B, A+/B+, and Pi 2 cases are different, so make sure that you get the right one. Figure 1-8 shows a Pi inside a typical case.

Figure 1-8

If you live somewhere hot, get a case with air holes to help keep your Pi cool and ventilated.

If you don't use a case, put your Pi on something that doesn't conduct electricity. Thick paper, cardboard, wood, plastic, glass, and ceramics (plates and such) are all fine. Baking trays, metal foil, cutlery, silver plate, and gold bars are all bad because they can create a short circuit.

If you're lucky, a short circuit will stop your Pi until you restart it. If you're not, it will kill your Pi dead forever. (Although if you have gold bars to spare, you can always buy another Pi. Or ten.)

Pi boards don't like static electricity. When you pick up a Pi board, hold it by the sides or by a USB or network socket. Don't prod the electronics with your fingers. Don't keep your Pi on the carpet or drag it over carpet. (Also, don't put it in the microwave and turn the power on, dissolve it in acid, or feed it to sharks. But you knew that anyway, huh?)

If you don't want to spend money on a case, you can print a case using cardboard! See www.raspberrypi.org/the-punnet-a-card-case-for-you-to-print-for-free.

Add WiFi (or not)

If you want to add WiFi, you have to plug a *WiFi dongle* — a small plastic stick with a USB plug at one end and WiFi electronics at the other — into a USB port.

There are many different dongles. Some are compatible with the Pi. Some aren't. Some start working and then stop for no reason. Others don't work at all. Some work almost all of the time but give you a very slow connection. This can drive you nuts. To stay happy, use a long Ethernet cable instead of WiFi.

Add a camera

A camera is a popular Pi extra. Most USB webcams work just fine with the Pi, but very old or very cheap webcams (less than $10) may not.

The official Pi Camera module is another option. It's a tiny electronic board with an even tinier camera that works better than you expect it to. The Pi comes with ready-made software for the camera, so — unlike a webcam — you don't have to write your own.

The camera is quite delicate, and if you use it a lot, you'll want to put your Pi and the camera inside a special camera-friendly case. Search the web for Pi camera case for the latest options.

The official Pi Camera comes in two types: standard and noIR, which is short for no infrared filter. You can use the noIR camera to make spooky ghostcam photos and videos using invisible infrared light. Most people buy the standard model. If you want to make a wildlife camera or hunt ghosts, get the noIR version.

Add loudspeakers and headphones

The Pi has a standard audio jack socket, like the ones on many mobile phones and MP3 players. You can plug a pair of speakers or headphones into the socket. If the Pi makes some noise, you'll hear it.

Because the Pi doesn't have built-in Bluetooth, it won't work with a Bluetooth speaker. It also doesn't work with Apple or Android phone docks.

Collect Parts the Lazy Way

The smart way to buy a Pi system is to buy a Pi Starter Kit from a Pi shop. The right Pi kit will have everything you need, except a monitor/TV and (usually) a monitor cable. Search online for Raspberry Pi Starter Kit to find the latest deals.

Some Starter Kits include a Model B instead of a B+. Check this so that you know what you're getting. Be careful to buy a Starter Kit, not an Electronics Kit; some shops sell kits of electronic parts for Pi projects. You may want one later, but you can't start with one! Make sure that your kit includes a power supply, keyboard, mouse, memory card, and cables.

If you have a mouse and keyboard already, see whether you can find a kit with just a Pi, a memory card, and a power supply. Some stores sell them, and they're cheaper than a full kit.

Check what you've got

If you don't want to buy a kit, many families have an old computer parts box or shelf. It's usually in the corner of an attic, garage, den, or spare room. To save money, raid the shelf and see what you find. You'll often discover old mice and keyboards, cables, and perhaps even an old monitor.

If your family doesn't have one, you can try asking uncles and aunts. Or you can get together with your friends to see what they've got!

Table 1-2 is a list of Pi parts. You can check off items as you find them or buy them.

Table 1-2	A Handy Pi System Checklist		
Extra	**Do I Need One?**	**Can I Find a Spare One?**	**Do I Need to Buy One?**
Monitor or TV	Yes		
USB Hub	Only for a Model A/B		
2A USB Hub Power Supply	Only for a Model A/B		
USB Keyboard	Yes		
USB Mouse	Yes		
2A Power Supply	Yes		
SDHC Memory Card	Only for a Model A/B		
Micro SDHC Memory Card	Only for a Model A+/B+/2		
Card Reader/Writer	Only if your Mac/PC doesn't have one already		
Ethernet Cable	Yes		

(continued)

Table 1-2 (continued)

Extra	Do I Need One?	Can I Find a Spare One?	Do I Need to Buy One?
WiFi Dongle	Only if you can't use an Ethernet cable		
HDMI to HDMI cable	Depends on monitor/ TV		
HDMI to DVI cable	Depends on monitor/ TV		
Case	Nice to have		
Camera	Nice to have		

Create a Mind for Your Pi

Without a mind, your Raspberry Pi is a useless blob of electronics.

Computer minds are very simple. An ant brain is a genius compared to a computer mind. But your Pi won't work at all without a mind, so you have to install a mind before you can use your Pi for fun.

In this chapter, you discover how to install a mind.

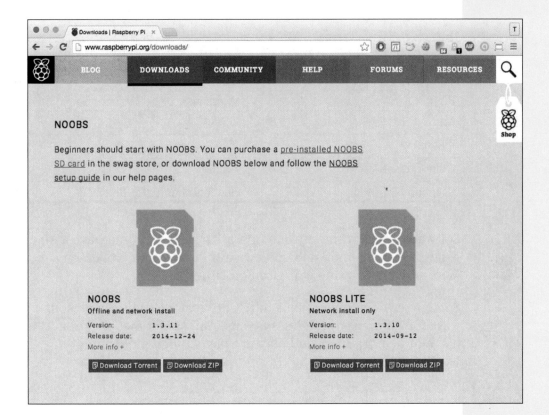

Understand Operating Systems

In computer-speak, the mind that runs your Pi is called an *operating system* (*OS* for short).

Operating systems are like a computer manager; they run your computer for you. When you tell your computer to do something, it's the OS that listens to your commands, makes them happen, and shows you what happens after you give them.

The OS includes the features that make the keyboard, mouse, screen, and storage work. It also connects your computer to the Internet and exchanges information with it.

Different kinds of computers have different operating systems. Table 2-1 lists the most popular kinds.

Table 2-1	Popular Operating Systems
Computer	**OS**
PC	Windows
Mac	OS X
iPhone	iOS
Other phones	Android
Raspberry Pi	See this chapter for details

Software works with only one operating system. If you have a Mac game, it won't run on a PC. Likewise, a PC game won't run on a Mac, and an iOS game won't run on either.

Sometimes developers make different versions of the same software for different operating systems. And sometimes they don't; it's a lot of extra work and may not pay enough money to be worth the time.

Meet Linux on the Pi

The bad news for Raspberry Pi fans is that you can't set up a Pi with Windows, OS X, iOS, or Android.

There is a version of Android for the Pi, but it doesn't work very well. So just pretend there isn't.

Instead of Windows or OS X, you can run a free OS called Linux on your Pi. Linux is unusual because it's designed for people who like to tinker with computers. You can change any feature of Linux to make it work the way you want.

Microsoft has promised to release a free version of Windows 10 for the Pi 2. But it's a cut-down version of Windows designed for hardware projects and not the full version that can run Office and the usual other stuff. This plan may change in the future, but for now, assume that Windows on the Pi won't be anything like Windows on a big PC.

Linux comes with free tools that help you get started with programming. When you install Linux on your Pi, you get the tools for free. And you get a lot of other software, also for free.

Because Linux is easy to modify, people keep changing it, so there are many different versions. Some versions are designed to do one thing well, like playing movies and music and running a media library. Others are designed for general computer use.

Changing Linux is hard, even if you're a computer expert. You need a lot of experience with computer programming before you can make changes without breaking anything. But even so — you can't change Windows or OS X no matter how much experience you have because the companies that make these operating systems don't let you.

Meet Raspbian

Your Pi uses an operating system called *Raspbian.* Raspbian is a special raspberry-flavored remix of a popular version of Linux called Debian.

The Raspbian desktop, shown in Figure 2-1, looks a bit like the desktop that appeared in older versions of Windows, before Windows 8 added bright tiles.

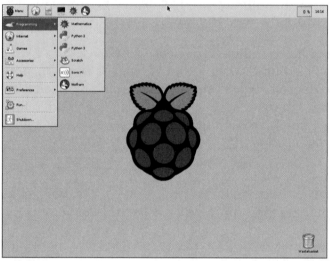

Figure 2-1

If you buy a memory card and run NOOBS and you find your desktop is white, not gray, you have an older version. Most of the stuff in this book will still work, but some menus and doodads are in different places. Really, you should wipe your card and copy the latest version of NOOBS to it anyway to get the latest, freshest version.

Raspbian also looks a bit like the OS X desktop, but without the flat gray highlights and the stylish lettering.

If you've used a desktop on a Mac or PC, Raspbian will feel familiar. There are some differences, which I cover in Chapter 5. But one desktop is a lot like another desktop, so you won't have to learn a whole lot of new stuff.

Debian was named after two Linux fans called Deb and Ian. (You don't need to remember this.)

Debian is popular because it works well for general computing. It doesn't include all the latest tinkering that happens around Linux, so it doesn't break as often as some versions of Linux do.

But it includes all the usual free Linux tools and software. The Raspberry Pi version also includes some free games.

Meet NOOBS

To set up your Pi with Raspbian, you have to use something called NOOBS. *NOOBS* (New Out Of the Box Software — but NOOTBS didn't work, so NOOBS it is) is a free tool for installing operating systems. To set up your Pi, follow these steps.

1. **Buy a memory card with NOOBS on it or save a dollar or two and follow the steps in this chapter to copy NOOBS to a card.**

   You can find the steps in the sections "Copy NOOBS on a Mac" and "Copy NOOBS on a PC" later in this chapter.

2. **Plug the memory card into your Pi.**

3. **Power up the Pi.**

4. **Follow the instructions shown by NOOBS to install Raspbian.**

5. **Restart the Pi.**

6. **Use Raspbian from then on.**

After you follow these steps, NOOBS hides. It's still on the memory card, but your Pi ignores it and launches straight into Raspbian, as if that's all it's ever known.

You can make NOOBS appear again if you power up your Pi with a special magic keyboard combo. You don't usually need to do this.

Get NOOBS the lazy way

If you bought a Pi starter kit with a memory card, it probably came with NOOBS already on it. If you didn't, you can buy cards with NOOBS from various suppliers by searching for — go on, you can guess — NOOBS.

When you have a card, you're done with this chapter. You can skip the rest!

 Make sure you buy the right card. If you buy the wrong card, it won't fit in your Pi, and you won't be able to use NOOBS or Raspbian. For a Model A or B Pi, buy an SD card, or a microSD card with an SD adaptor. For a Model A+ or B+ Pi or a Pi 2, buy a microSD card. (If it comes with an adaptor, keep it — it may be useful later.)

Get NOOBS the Hard Way

 If you don't want to buy a NOOBS card, you can make your own.

Problem! Setting up a memory card with NOOBS is a chore. You have to do a lot of downloading and copying and installing and waiting.

It isn't hard, but it is booooooooooring.

So it's a *really* good idea to get a ready-made card. If you want to make your own anyway, you need

- **A free PC or Mac**

- **A memory card that fits your Pi**

- **A card reader that matches your memory card**

- **Free software from the Internet**

- **An hour or two**

Find a PC or Mac

This part is easy. Any Mac or PC less than five years old will do. Older models may still be fine. But the older your computer, the more likely you are to have problems with the instructions in the rest of this chapter.

Choose a memory card

You need a card that matches your Pi. A or B boards take an SD card or a microSD card with an SD adaptor. A+, B+, and Pi 2 boards take a microSD card. Chapter 1 has more information about where to buy cards and which cards to buy. Figure 2-2 shows the memory cards that work with the Pi. As a bonus, Figure 2-2 also includes an adaptor that allows a microSD card to work in an SD slot.

Figure 2-2

Choose a card reader

Some Mac and PC models have memory card slots built into the front, back, or side. If you're lucky, the slot — or one of the slots, if there's more than one — will match your card.

If you're not so lucky, you need to buy or find an external card reader. Figure 2-3 shows an example. Card readers have a USB plug at one end and some card slots in a box at the other. You can find them online, at any office supply store, or in many supermarkets. They cost around $10.

The box in Figure 2-3 is big and square. Most readers look flatter and thinner (except the big and square ones).

Figure 2-3

There are eleventy million billion different kinds of memory cards. (Actually there are about 20, so it's not that bad.) Most readers work with SD cards. Not quite as many work with microSD cards.

Get a reader with the right slots. Otherwise, you'll have to take it back and buy another.

Use a card reader

To use a reader, plug the USB connector into a spare USB socket on your Mac or PC. Plug in your blank memory card. It appears as an external hard disk in Finder on the Mac or in File Manager in Windows.

And, er, that's it. Almost. . . . Before you can install NOOBS, you have to format the card. This magic process prepares your card so that it works with the Pi.

Set up NOOBS on a memory card

The steps for setting up NOOBS on a memory card are the same on a Mac and a PC, but some of the details are different. You need to

1. **Download and install free formatting software.**

2. **Use the software to format (prepare) your memory card.**

3. **Download NOOBS.**

4. **Extract the files in NOOBS to a folder.**

5. **Copy the files to the memory card.**

6. **Eject the card safely.**

7. **Remove the card from the reader.**

Your card now has NOOBS on it. When you plug in your card and power up your Pi, NOOBS runs, and you can install Raspbian.

If you're thinking this is a lot of work to set up a toy computer, it is. It would be good if the Pi foundation sold cards with Raspbian pre-installed, so you could skip NOOBS and just get on with using your Pi. For some reason, it doesn't. (Oh, well.)

You can use standard Windows and OS X tools to format a memory card. This approach often works, but sometimes it doesn't. It's best to use the official tool, available from a site called `http://sdcard.org`, to prepare your card.

Download the SD formatter to a Mac

You need to download the SD formatter to a Mac only once. If you want to make more cards with NOOBS on them, you can skip this section after the first card.

1. **Open a web browser and view**
   `www.sdcard.org/downloads/formatter_4`.

2. **Scroll down the page until you see the big blue download buttons shown in Figure 2-4.**

3. **Click the Download SD Formatter for Mac button.**

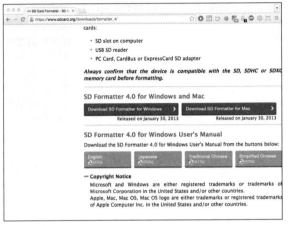

Figure 2-4

4. **Download the .pkg file to your Mac.**

5. **Double-click the .pkg file and follow the installation instructions.**

6. **Open /Applications and find SDFormatter.app.**

Format a memory card on a Mac

The formatter is very simple. To use it, change a few options and click Format. Follow these steps:

1. **If you're using an external card reader, plug your card into your reader and then plug the reader into a spare USB slot on your Mac; if your Mac has a built-in reader, plug the card into it.**

2. **Double-click SDFormatter.app to start it.**

3. **Enter your password and click OK.**

4. **When the window shown in Figure 2-5 appears, select your card from the menu near the top.**

You need to do this step only if you have more than one card.

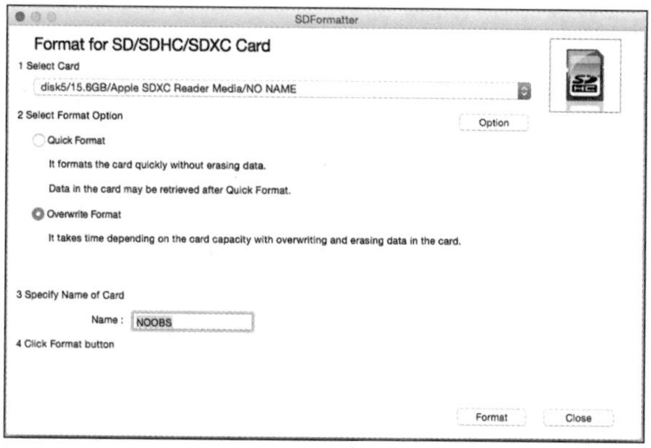

Figure 2-5

If no cards appear, make sure that you connected your reader correctly and pushed the card all the way into a reader slot.

If you have more than one card — you probably don't, but just in case — make sure that you pick the right one. Formatting a card removes all the information for it, forever.

5. **Type NOOBS into the Name box.**

   You can skip this step. The card name doesn't matter. But it's useful to name your cards so that you know what's on them.

6. **Click the Option button and select Yes in the Logical Address Adjustment box.**

   I have no idea what this option does. But everyone says you should do it.

7. **Click OK to close the box.**

8. **Click the tiny circle next to Overwrite Format about halfway down.**

   Technically, this tiny circle is called a *radio button*. It doesn't really use radio, so the name doesn't make a lot of sense. But that's what it's called.

9. **Click Format and wait.**

It can take ten minutes or so to format a card. The time depends on the card size, card speed, weather conditions, phase of the moon, and so on. The formatter shows a progress bar as it works so you can see whether you have time to goof off and do something fun before it finishes.

10. **Click Close when the formatter is done.**

You have a blank memory card, and you've set it up so that your Pi can read it. Now you can copy NOOBS to it.

Download NOOBS to a Mac

NOOBS is available from the Raspberry Pi Foundation site, shown in Figure 2-6. The current URL is `www.raspberrypi.org/downloads`.

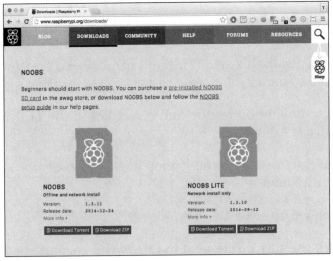

Figure 2-6

NOOBS comes in two versions. The standard version includes Raspbian. The Lite version downloads Raspbian from the Internet before it installs it. The standard version works even if your Pi isn't connected to the Internet, so it's a better choice.

Click the Download ZIP button shown in Figure 2-6 and download the file to your Mac. Remember the download location.

The default download location is /Downloads in your user folder. Your browser may download the file to a different location, depending on how it's set up. It may also ask you where to save the file. If you're lucky, it will show a hotlink to the downloaded file at the bottom of the browser window. If you're not, you'll have to work out where the file is yourself.

NOOBS is a huge file. It's more than 720MB! It takes a long time to download. If you have slow broadband, you may have to leave it downloading overnight, especially if the rest of your family wants to use the Internet during the day.

Extract NOOBS on a Mac

To extract the files, double-click the file you downloaded. It should have zip on the end. When you double-click the file, Finder creates a folder with all the files that were squashed inside it.

Figure 2-7 shows how this process works. The folder is open to show the files inside. You can see the original zip file under the files.

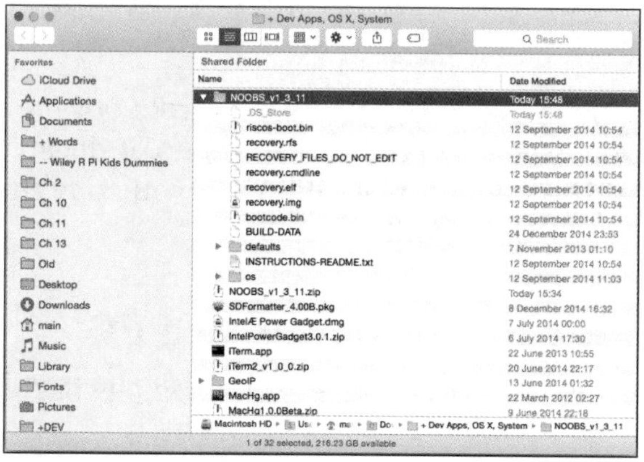

Figure 2-7

Copy NOOBS on a Mac

To copy NOOBS to the card, open a new Finder window and open the card. It should appear in the list of Devices, which is often at the bottom of finder.

Select the files in the NOOBS folder. You can shift-click to select them all at once. Drag them from the NOOBS folder to the NOOBS card, as shown in Figure 2-8.

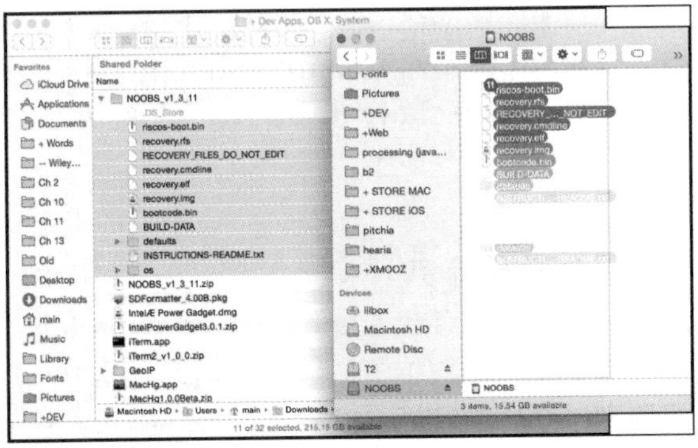

Figure 2-8

When you release the mouse, Finder copies them to the card. Click the Eject icon to eject the card and pull it out of your Mac or your reader. Now you can plug the card into your Pi — after you connect it up.

WARNING! Don't just drag the NOOBS folder to your card! *Copy the files inside the NOOBS folder.* When the Pi starts up, it doesn't know how to look inside a folder for NOOBS. So if you copy the folder and not the files, NOOBS won't work.

Download the SD formatter to a PC

The instructions for a PC are similar to the Mac instructions. But there are some differences:

1. **Open a web browser and view**
   `www.sdcard.org/downloads/formatter_4/`.

2. Scroll down the page until you see the big blue download buttons, shown in Figure 2-9.

Figure 2-9

3. Click the Download SD Formatter for Windows button.

4. Download the zip file to your PC.

5. Double-click the zip file.

6. Double click setup.exe when it appears in File Manager.

7. Follow the instructions to install the formatter.

When you're done, a Formatter icon appears on your desktop.

Formatting a memory card on a PC

The PC formatter version of the formatter app has the same options as the Mac version, but they're in slightly different places in the app's window.

To format a card, follow these steps:

1. If you're using an external card reader, plug your card into your reader and then plug the reader into a spare USB slot on your PC; if your PC has a built-in reader, plug the card into it.

2. Double-click the SDFormatter icon on the desktop to start it.

3. When the window shown in Figure 2-10 appears, select your card from the Drive menu.

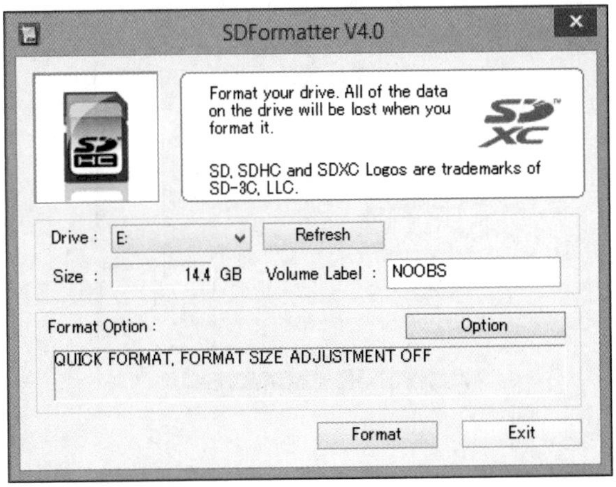

Figure 2-10

Make sure that you select the right drive. Check the Size box to make sure that you're not about to format your system drive. The number should be more or less the same as the number of GB on your card. If you format your system drive, you will break your PC, and everyone will get really mad at you. There will be a lot of angry shouting, and you don't want that. Double-check the drive selection and then double-check it again, just to be sure.

4. Type NOOBS into the Volume Label box.

5. Click Option.

6. In the Option Setting dialog box shown in Figure 2-11, select FULL (OverWrite) in the FORMAT TYPE drop-down list.

7. Select ON in the FORMAT SIZE ADJUSTMENT drop-down list.

8. Click OK.

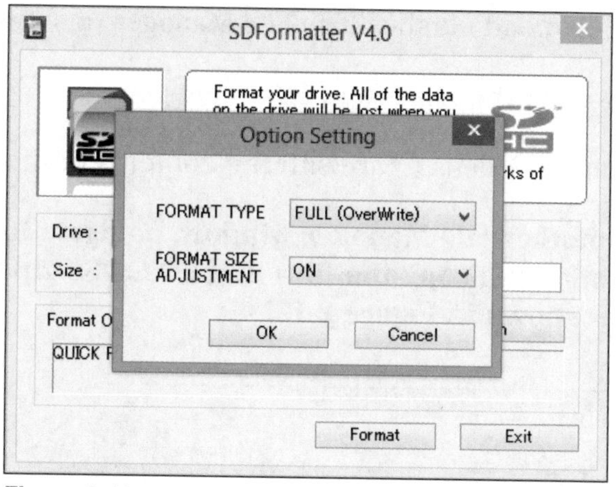

Figure 2-11

9. Check again that you selected the drive letter that matches your memory card and not a hard disk full of photos, emails, and other family records that can never, ever be replaced.

10. If you're really sure that you selected the drive that matches your memory card, click Format.

11. Go find something else to do away from the PC while the formatter formats the card.

12. Click OK to close the window that tells you that formatting is complete.

13. Click Exit to quit the formatter.

Download NOOBS to a PC

NOOBS doesn't care whether you're using a Mac or a PC, so you can go straight to www.raspberrypi.org/downloads and download the standard version. Remember the download location.

After the download finishes, use File Manager to show the zip file:

1. **Double-click the zip file in File Manager.**

   File Manager opens a tab with the contents of the zip file.

2. **Open another File Manager window, navigate to the card drive, and drag-copy the files in the NOOBS zip file to the card, as shown in Figure 2-12.**

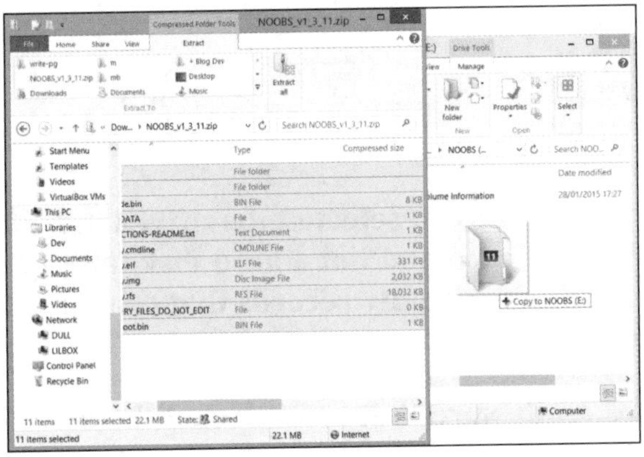

Figure 2-12

3. **In your taskbar, click the tiny triangle that points upward.**

   It's usually next to the keyboard icon.

4. **In the box that appears, click the tiny icon that looks like a USB cable with a green checkmark next to it.**

   It's often too small to see, but Figure 2-13 should give you a clue. The Eject Hardware tooltip shown in Figure 2-13 gives you another hint.

5. **Click EJECT NOOBS in the list that appears.**

   The drive letter appears after EJECT NOOBS so that you can be sure you're ejecting the right drive.

You can now pull the card out of the reader and get ready to use it in your Pi.

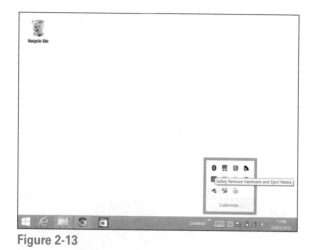

Figure 2-13

3

Connect Your Pi

It isn't hard to connect up a Pi system. If you never move your Pi, you only have to do it once. After that, you can leave everything connected.

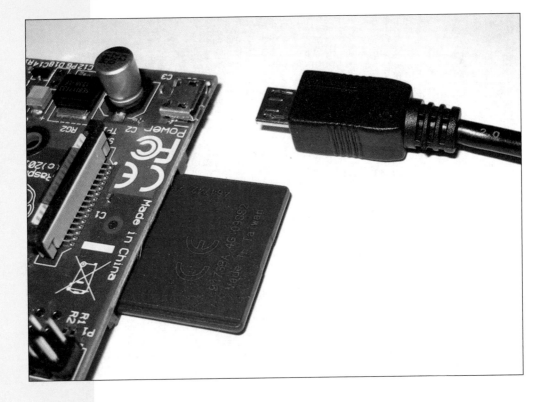

Find a Space

If your Pi system is ready and waiting in a big — but organized — pile, you're ready to get it working. (If it's not, see the checklist in Chapter 1.)

Start by finding a flat space on a desk with enough space for a monitor, mouse, and keyboard. You probably need more space than you think, so grab the biggest space you can find.

If you can't find a desk, maybe you can set up on the floor. It won't be as comfortable as a desk, but it will do to get started, as long as you get a desk soon and remember not to tread on the Pi by accident.

Some people like to use a kitchen table for computer experiments. Kitchen tables are big and flat, but kitchens are used for cooking and eating, so you probably won't be able to keep your Pi set up. If you really can't find anywhere else in the house, check with the grown-ups whether it's okay to use the kitchen before setting up.

Find the Power

No, using a Pi won't make you a superhero — not unless you count programming and game skills as superpowers.

Computers need electricity, and all the parts of a Pi system need their own power sockets.

You usually need at least one, maybe more, power strips. A *power strip* has a plug on one end of a cable. The other end holds a plastic block with a row of power sockets. You need a strip long enough to run from a wall socket to your desk, and you also need enough sockets for all the parts. Six should be enough.

If you don't already have enough power strips, go find some now. (If you don't have any spare ones at home, you may have to buy them.)

Plug in and set up the power strip before you do anything else. Put the strips by the side of your desk if you can, so you don't have to crawl around the desk with a flashlight. (At best, you'll bump your head. At worst, you'll be eaten by evil scary desk monsters. Also, dust bunnies. . . .)

In the UK, power strips are sometimes called *four-ways* because most have four sockets. (Six-way and eight-way strips are still called four-ways, because they are.) Some power strips have special electronics inside them to help keep computers safe if — for example — your house is struck by lightning. These extra-technical super-strips are a lot more expensive than the normal cheap kind. You don't need them. (If your house is struck by lightning, you have more to worry about than keeping your Pi working.)

Plug in a Memory Card

Plug in your memory card first because it's easier when you have nothing else connected.

Here's a weird thing about the Pi: The memory card slot is under the board. The card sticks out the side. *And* it's upside down, with the pins at the top and the label at the bottom.

This location makes it easy to pull it in and out, but it looks kind of ugly and fragile.

Plug a card into a Model A or B

The older boards have a big card slot for a big SD card. Start with your Pi board and make sure that it's the right way up, with all the electronics on top. The power must be off.

Pick up the SD card and turn it over so you can see the metal pins at one end. Push the card with the pins first into the slot under the Pi board until it won't go any farther.

If it doesn't go in, make sure the pins are in the right place and try again. Don't force it!

Turn over the Pi board to check you've done it right. There should be no space between the card and the card slot, as in Figure 3-1.

Figure 3-1

You can turn the Pi board the right way up now.

The card slot on the A/B models sort of half-locks, kind of. It's easy to jiggle the card or pull it out by accident. This is *very* bad.

Try not to move your Pi board with the power on and the software running! Don't jiggle the card. And especially don't power up the Pi and then put the card in, or pull it out with the power on.

You'll probably break the Pi and the memory card, and everyone will be very sad, including you. And no one wants that.

Plug a card into a Model A+, B+, or Pi 2

To plug a card into a Model A+, B+, or Pi 2, follow the same steps for the newer Pi boards. The memory card and the slot are much smaller. (Refer to Chapter 1 to see what the memory card and slot look like.)

This card slot works better. The card locks when you push it in so that you can't pull it out by accident. Accidental jiggling isn't a problem.

If you need to remove the card, power down the Pi and disconnect the power. Push the card to unlock it. *Now* you can pull it out.

Connect a Monitor or TV

To connect a monitor or TV, put the monitor or TV near the back of your desk and turn it around so that you can see the connectors on the back.

If you read Chapter 1, you know you have two choices. The Pi end of the cable for the screen always has an HDMI connector.

The other end needs either an HDMI connector or a DVI connector, depending on what kind of screen/monitor/TV you have.

Use an HDMI-to-HDMI lead

If your monitor has an HDMI socket — you can tell because it's labeled HDMI — plug one end of your HDMI lead into the socket. Plug the other end into the HDMI connector on your Pi.

Figure 3-2 shows a Model B board. One end of the HDMI lead is free so that you can see what an HDMI lead looks like. This end plugs into your monitor.

Figure 3-2

The other end has the same connector. It goes into the big, flat HDMI socket at the back of the board.

The connector on a Model A+/B+/2 board looks the same and works the same way. It's more or less in the same place on the board.

The metal boxes in the middle of the photo are the Ethernet/network connector and USB slots. They're only shown in Figure 3-2 because they were in the way, and not because they have anything to do with HDMI — they don't. It was near impossible to take a good photo of the HDMI lead and connector without including them. But you got a free close-up of them, which can't be bad.

Use an HDMI-to-DVI adaptor lead

If your monitor has a DVI socket, you need an HDMI/DVI adaptor cable. (Chapter 1 has more details.)

Figure 3-2 shows a photo. It's the same deal as Figure 3-1. The HDMI end plugs into the HDMI connector on the Pi. The other end — the end that plugs into a monitor — is floating.

Figure 3-3

There's one thing to know: an HDMI plug just works. You push it in, and it locks.

If you push in a DVI plug, it falls out again. Always.

See that screw on the DVI plug? See the finger bolts behind the body of the plug? There are screws on both sides. You have to screw them in tight to stop the plug from falling out.

Turn on monitor power

When you're all connected up, plug the power lead into the monitor/TV, and plug the lead into a socket on your power strip.

You can power up the monitor if you want. (It won't show anything interesting yet.)

Connect a USB Hub

If you have a Model A or Model B Pi board, you need a USB hub. (Chapter 1 has the full details for the hub, too.)

If you have a newer Model A+ or B+ Pi, you can skip this step because it should work fine without a hub.

Hubs come in all shapes and sizes. Some are round and flat, some are triangular, some are box-shaped, and a few are shaped like animals, plants, or people.

They all have a collection of USB sockets on the top/sides, a power socket, like the one in Figure 3-4, and a single USB plug. You should have a hub with a separate power supply. (If not, see Chapter 1.)

Push the USB plug into one of the USB sockets on your Pi. It doesn't matter which one; they all do the same thing.

Next, plug the power supply into your power strip. Some hubs have a fixed power cable. If you have one of these, you're done.

Others have a power socket. (There are literally about 15 different types.) Plug the power lead into the matching socket on the hub.

And that's it.

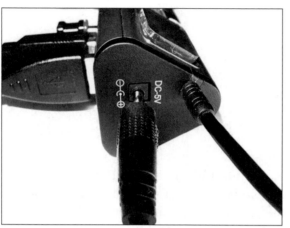

Figure 3-4

 Power sockets often have a label like 5V DC. Sometimes there's a diagram showing details about the plug/socket. USB sockets don't have this label. Sometimes they have a squiggly symbol with tiny circles and a box and an arrow.

 If you're using a hub and a Model A/B, connect all USB accessories through the hub, including the keyboard, mouse, and anything else with a WiFi plug. Don't plug anything else into the Pi! If you do, it will run out of power and stop working.

Connect a Keyboard and Mouse

Connecting a keyboard and mouse to your Pi is easy. On a Model A+/B+/2, plug the flat USB connector from the keyboard into a USB socket on the Pi board. Then do the same for the mouse.

With a Model B or A, plug the connectors into a hub instead, as in the previous section.

 By the time you've added a mouse, keyboard, and maybe a hub, your desk will be disappearing under a mess of cables. It's a good idea to bundle each cable and wrap the end around the bundle a couple of times to keep the wiring neater.

Connect to the Internet

Most homes have a *router* — a box that connects to the Internet. Most routers have at least one spare Ethernet socket.

To connect your Pi to the Internet, plug your Ethernet cable into the Ethernet socket on your Pi. (It's the big socket that isn't a USB.)

Plug the other end into the router, as shown in Figure 3-5. All routers are different, so your router probably won't look like this one. Cables are different, too. Some are round and thick; some are flat and thin (not many are round and thin, but there's probably one somewhere, just to be difficult).

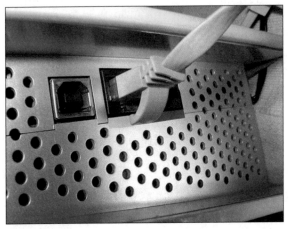

Figure 3-5

The sockets are always the same, though.

Connect Power

Figure 3-6 shows a typical Pi power adaptor, introduced in Chapter 1, plugged into a UK power strip. (A U.S. power strip has round holes instead of the rectangular ones here. Otherwise, no diff.)

Figure 3-6

Some Pi power adaptors have one or two USB sockets. Others just have a cable running out of the adaptor.

They all work more or less the same way. Plug in the adaptor. It starts working.

If your adaptor has two sockets, don't use the other socket! Your Pi wants all the power it can get. It doesn't like sharing.

Figure 3-7 shows what happens at the other end. The cable needs an extra-special tiny microUSB connector, which plugs into the microUSB socket on the Pi board.

Just to confuse you, there's more than one kind of tiny USB plug. A miniUSB plug looks very similar, but it won't fit into the Pi no matter how hard you force it — not even after you break the Pi board and/or the connector. Make sure that you get the right kind of cable. Only a microUSB will do.

On the Model A/B, the socket is close to the memory card along one edge. On the Model A+/B+/Pi 2, it's next to the HDMI connector at the top of the board. (Or the bottom, if you turn the board around.)

Figure 3-7

 If you look at the Pi board up close, you'll see the power socket is labeled PWR IN on the Pi 2, PWR on the A+/B+, and POWER on the A/B. The letters are really tiny, though!

There's no power switch! It was left out to make the Pi as cheap as possible and to save space on the board.

You're ready to power up your Pi. Good job! But don't do it yet! You need to know more about setting up and powering down the Pi before you do.

 The microUSB socket isn't very strong. If you keep plugging the power cable in and out, the socket breaks. It's better to plug and unplug the adaptor from your power strip. Leave the microUSB end of the cable plugged in all the time. Another option is to get a USB socket to USB plug extender cable, leave one end permanently plugged into the adaptor, the other end plugged into the Pi, and connect the plug/socket in the middle when you want power.

Power Up and Get Started

It's exciting starting your Pi for the first time, but you have to do some extra work before you can start using it. Don't worry — it's not hard, and you only have to do it once.

When **Raspbian** boots up you will need to log in to the system.

The default username for **Raspbian** is **pi**, with the default password **raspberry**.

You will need to remember this information to log in so you might want to write it down now.

Raspbian: Extracting filesystem

1%

25 MB of 2320 MB written (0.5 MB/sec)

Power Up Your Pi

If you followed all the steps in Chapter 3, you're ready to power up your Pi. (If not, go there now.)

1. **Plug the adaptor into a power socket.**

   If the socket/four-way/power strip has switches, make sure they're on.

   Life! Action! Things should happen on the screen. If you set up NOOBS correctly, you should see something like Figure 4-1, with a list of options.

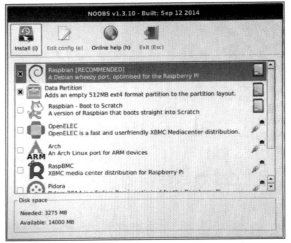

Figure 4-1: Starting NOOBs for the first time.

Figures 4-1 and 4-2 are fuzzier than usual because they're actual photos of a screen, taken with a camera — an iPhone 6, if you really want to know. There's no easy way to take the usual computer screen shots of NOOBS.

2. **When you see the screen, use the mouse — you did remember to plug it in, right? — to click the two top checkboxes.**

   You want the ones that say Raspbian [RECOMMENDED] and Data Partition.

3. **Click the Install button at the top left or press i on your keyboard.**

4. **Click Yes when the Pi asks whether you want to overwrite the memory card OMG blah blah techno-blah.**

   (It's fine to overwrite the card. Really.)

   You see the screen in Figure 4-2. The Pi starts installing Raspbian. If you have nothing else to do, you can watch the progress bar at the bottom of the screen. It takes 10 to 15 minutes to finish and the messages it shows aren't all that interesting, so you may as well go do something fun while you're waiting.

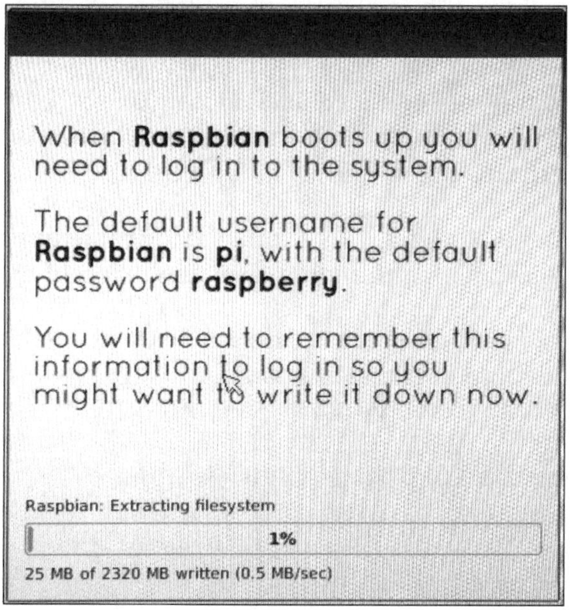

When **Raspbian** boots up you will need to log in to the system.

The default username for **Raspbian** is **pi**, with the default password **raspberry**.

You will need to remember this information to log in so you might want to write it down now.

Raspbian: Extracting filesystem

1%

25 MB of 2320 MB written (0.5 MB/sec)

Figure 4-2: Watching as NOOBS installs Raspbian.

5. **Make a note of the details on this screen — the username** pi **and the password** raspberry.

You need them when you start using your Pi. If you forget them, your Pi won't let you use it, and that will be *very* bad.

Boot Raspbian

After NOOBS finishes, your Pi restarts automatically. This time, it doesn't start NOOBS. It starts — the technical word is *boots* — Raspbian.

It's called booting because it's short for pulling yourself up by your bootstraps, which is what the startup sequence was called in computer prehistory. Of course, you can't actually pull yourself up by pulling on your boots, because you're standing on them. Adding straps doesn't fix this — even if most boots had straps, which they don't. Powering up would have been too simple, I guess.

Has NOOBS gone? Mostly. From now on, if you don't touch anything while the Pi boots, you'll see Raspbian.

The Raspbian boot sequence lists a lot more stuff on the screen than NOOBS does. You get a complete list of everything Raspbian is doing, with details, as shown in Figure 4-3.

You don't need to watch this sequence, or remember it, or pay any attention to it — although it does look kind of cool.

If you're an expert Linux user, you can learn something about the settings and state of Linux by reading this text as it scrolls by. ("Ooh look — the keyboard just connected".)

If you're not — no big. None of it is essential.

Figure 4-3: Looking at the boot sequence and the command prompt.

The important part happens at the end, when all the scrolling stops. You'll see a message about Debian/Linux at the very end, and under that is a line of green and blue text that looks like this (without the green and blue):

```
pi@raspberrypi ~ $
```

After it, you can see a flashing green rectangle.

This is the *command prompt.* Because the Pi is an old-fashioned computer, you can tell it what to do by typing commands on your keyboard.

Mouse? No. Menus? Uh. Keyboard typing only.

The prompt tells you the Pi is waiting for your command. It also reminds you that your name on the Pi is pi, and that the computer is called raspberrypi — just in case you've forgotten already.

Some commands take a while to work. If you can't see the prompt, there's no point typing a command. The Pi is still thinking about the last thing you told it to do. It's not ready to do something else yet.

You can find out more about the command prompt and the Linux commands you can use in Chapters 5, 10, and 11.

Configure Your Pi

This chapter introduces exactly one command, but it's a very important one. You can use the command to change important settings in your Pi — which is sometimes called changing or setting the configuration.

Type the following and then press the Enter key:

```
sudo raspi-config
```

Make sure that you use small letters and not big letters (lowercase not uppercase) and type a minus sign (also known as a *hyphen*) between the two words.

Don't add any extra spaces or miss adding the space between `sudo` and the rest of the command.

When you type commands at the command line, they have to be 100 percent right. You can't make *any* mistakes — no extra letters, no extra spaces, no wrong letters, no big letters when you should use small letters. Otherwise, the Pi won't understand what you're trying to do.

Use the Setup options

If you don't make any mistakes, you see a screen like the one in Figure 4-4. This screen is a menu. It's like a clumsy and hard-to-use version of the drop-down menus you see in apps on a Mac or a PC.

You can't click on things with your mouse. You have to select them by using the up/down arrow keys on your keyboard. Then you press the Enter key to select them.

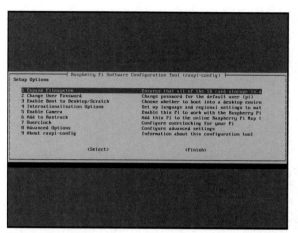

Figure 4-4: Setting up . . . stuff with the raspi-config command.

Try it now. Press the down arrow, and the red bar moves down by one item. Press the up arrow, and it moves up by one item.

To access the two lower options — they're <Select> and <Finish> on this screen, but you'll see other words on other screens — use the left and right arrows to highlight them. Press Enter to select them.

If you didn't use NOOBS to make Raspbian, select 1 Expand Filesystem first. Press Enter and follow the instructions.

Otherwise, move the red highlight down to 4 Internationalisation Options and press the Enter key.

The items you see in the Setup options keep changing. You may not see exactly the same list you see here. If you don't know what something does, leave it alone!

Set the locale

After you select the Internationalisation option, the screen changes to the one in Figure 4-5.

1. **Press Enter again to set the locale.**

   The screen switches back to the command prompt, and you'll start to worry that you've done the wrong thing.

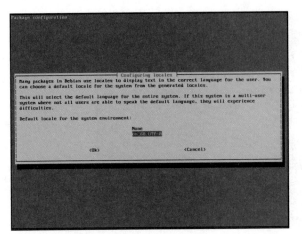

Figure 4-5: Setting the default locale.

You haven't. The local configuration page takes a few seconds to load. Don't panic until it appears. (And don't panic then either. Everything is fine.)

A *locale* is a lot like a location where you live or work, but sounds more clever. It's a language setting. It changes the language and spelling you see. A lot of software ignores it, but you'll set it anyway.

You see a red box next to an item labeled All locales.

2. **Press Enter.**

You see another screen like the one in Figure 4-5.

3. **Make sure that en_GB.UTF-8 is highlighted and press Enter again.**

The local screen goes away for a while, the Pi does some thinking, and eventually you end up back at the screen you saw in Figure 4-4.

Your Pi now speaks UK English.

Why can't you set U.S. English? In the current version of the software, you don't get a choice. This is what's called a *bug* — a mistake in the software.

It may get fixed in a future version, so you can try using the down arrow key to scroll the red box down from All Locales before pressing Enter and see whether it changes anything. If you're in the U.S., scroll it down to en-US.UTF8 UTF8.

UTF8 is short for Universal Character Set + Transformation Format 8. It doesn't look like it has enough letters, but it does. UTF is a way of setting up text on a computer so that it can show symbols and letters from other languages. This can get so complicated it makes grown-up programmers cry and wail, so I won't say any more about it here.

Understand time zones

Your Pi needs to know what time it is. It reads the time from the Internet when you boot it, so you don't need to set the hours, minutes and seconds, or the date. But you do need to tell it where you live so that it can adjust for your time zone.

If you're in the United States, you probably know about time zones already. If you're in the UK, you maybe know about summer time, and you may or may not know about European and other times.

Time zones work like this: The Earth is round and it spins. So if you use the sun as a clock, it's a different time everywhere around the earth. In some places, the sun is overhead. In others, it's rising. In others, it's setting. And for half the world, it's night time.

It would be convenient if everyone used the same clock time. But it wouldn't make a lot of sense. For some people, 3 p.m. would be early morning. For others, it would still be night, or midday, or sunset.

Time zones were invented to fix this problem. There's one reference time, based on a line through both poles through a place near London called Greenwich. This is called *Greenwich Mean Time* (GMT).

The line that marks GMT is part of a museum called the Royal Observatory. It has telescopes and bits of old satellites and other fun science things. At night, the line is marked by a laser that shoots across London. If you're in the UK, it's a cool place to visit.

Around GMT are wide zones offset by some whole number of hours. In the U.S., *Eastern Standard Time* covers the eastern states and is five hours behind GMT. So when it's 6 p.m. in England, it's 1 p.m. in New York. *Central Time* covers the states north of Texas, Louisiana, and Alabama and is six hours behind. Then there's *Mountain Time* (seven hours) and *Pacific Time* (eight hours).

And then there are two more zones for Alaska (nine hours) and Hawaii.

Going the other way, some of Europe is 1 hour ahead of GMT, then as you go east it gets 2 hours ahead, then 3 hours, and eventually you get to New Zealand, which is 13 hours.

The point? Local time is sort-of based on sun position. When it's midday, the sun is overhead. When it's midnight, it's always dark.

But places still share times, so when it's midday where you live, it's midday where your friends live, too (unless you have friends all over the Internet). And you don't get to school an hour early or late. Which is a good thing. Mostly.

If you want to find out more, search the web for time zone map. A lot of the zones have kinks and wiggles at the edges for technical and political reasons. But you still get broad zones where the time is the same, and it's easy to work out the time difference from GMT.

Set the time zone

Why does setting the time zone matter for your Pi? Your Pi gets the date and time from the Internet when it boots up. It also adjusts for the one-hour offset of summer time automatically.

But it still needs to know your time zone, because the Pi doesn't know where you live.

To set the time zone, use the up/down arrow keys to select the Change Time Zone option in the Internationalisation Options. Then press Enter.

Then wait while the Time Zone option loads, which always takes longer than you expect.

The easy way to set the zone is to select your area from the list in Figure 4-6. Use the up/down arrow keys to highlight your area and press Enter to select it. Then scroll up and down a list of cities (if you pick Europe) or time zones (if you select the U.S.).

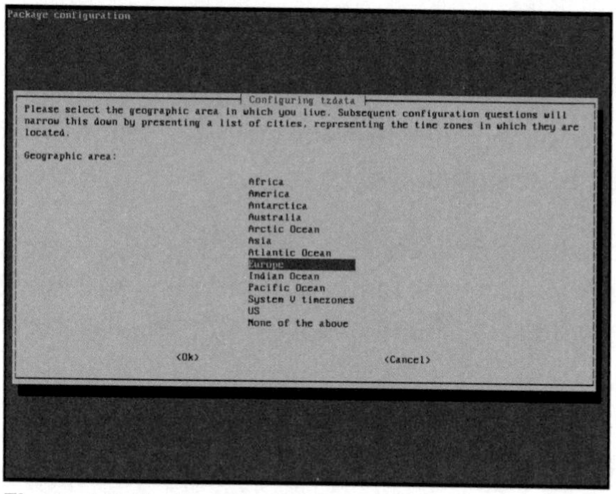

Figure 4-6: Setting the time zone.

You don't have to pick the city nearest to you. Pick one in the same time zone. For the UK, that means London. Press Enter.

For the United States, you get all the usual time zones and some extra ones you probably won't have heard of, like Starke County

(Indiana). Pick the right zone for where you live. If you're not sure what it is, ask a grown-up. Press Enter.

The Pi sets the time zone and then sends you back to the main Setup Options page.

Understand keyboard layouts

The keyboard-configuration option can drive you nuts. You'll probably be okay when you're done working through it. If you can't get it to work, you may need another keyboard.

The problem: There's more than one way to arrange the letters on a keyboard. Keyboard layouts are not standard. There are some semi-standard layouts, but they're not 100 percent everyone-does-it-this-way standard.

So you need to tell your Pi which layout your keyboard has. If you pick the wrong layout, the letters on the keys don't match the letters that appear when you press them.

For example, if you type @ to make an email address, you get a " instead.

If you get the keyboard selection very wrong, you won't be able to type some characters at all.

The vertical slash | character (also known as *pipe*) can be a real problem. It's very useful for Linux commands, but some keyboards don't include it. The only way to fix this is to use a different keyboard.

Set the keyboard layout

To set the keyboard layout:

1. **Select the Internationalisation Options and then select Option 3 — handily labeled Change Keyboard Layout.**

   After a very long wait — it's always longer than you expect — you'll see a screen like Figure 4-7. This is really just a long list of keyboards from all kinds of keyboard and computer makers.

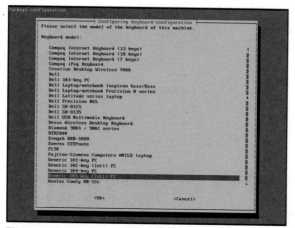

Figure 4-7: Picking a keyboard.

A lot of this list is junk. Some of the names, like the Amiga and the Atari TT, are computers from way back in time.

2. **To pick a layout, move the red highlight up and down until you see a name that matches the keyboard you have.**

   If you don't know the name, select the Generic 105-key (Intl) PC if you're in the UK, or the Generic 104-key PC if you're in the United States.

3. **Press Enter.**

4. **On the next screen, select the *default option* — in computer-speak, that's the one that's already selected for you — unless you have a Mac (for U.S.) or Mac International (for UK) keyboard, in which case select that instead.**

   The next best option is the Extended WinKeys, but don't try that yet.

5. **Press Enter.**

   Figure 4-8 shows the next screen. Most keyboards have a special key labeled AltGr, which is used for typing non-English characters with accents and extra squiggles.

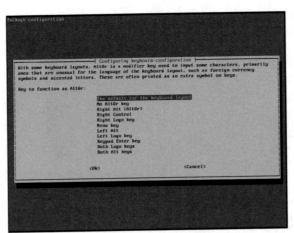

Figure 4-8: Dealing with the AltGr key, or one of the many alternatives.

6. **Choose "The default for the keyboard layout" option unless you've tried it already and it didn't work**

There are too many possibilities to list here. A smart first choice is to press Enter to select "The default for the keyboard layout option." If that one doesn't give you the right letters in the right places you can come back later and experiment with the other choices.

You can pick the default on the next page, too. It selects a key for a different set of complicated keyboard sequences to make an even wider selection of characters.

7. **If you're in the UK or the U.S., ignore the AltGr/Compose questions.**

You probably won't be typing emails in French or Polish on your Pi. If you need to, or if you move to France or Poland, you'll probably need to find a local expert to set all this up for you. There are experts who have worked with computers for years and still don't get how this stuff works.

8. **Finally, leave the <No> option selected for the question about the X Server and press Enter.**

   Wait while the Pi makes a keymap.

9. **Select the <Finish> option — use the right/left arrows and Enter — and try typing some of the less common characters on your keyboard.**

   If the @, ", ~, #, £/$ characters all work, you're probably okay.

10. **If all the characters don't work, use the** `sudo raspi-config` **command to go back into the Internationalisation Options and the Keyboard Configuration to pick a different keyboard layout.**

   If you can't get it to work after a couple of tries, go buy another keyboard with a different layout, and try again.

Set Up Advanced Options

You can use your Pi now. It should just work. You can run `sudo raspi-config` again if you want to change anything.

You can change some advanced settings if you want to, but you can also ignore them.

Set up overclocking

The original Pi was not a fast computer. The Pi 2 is faster, but still not as fast as a Mac or a PC.

You can make your Pi go faster by overclocking it. *Overclocking* is like pushing down the accelerator in a car. In computers, the clock ticks a few hundred million times a second. When you overclock, it ticks more often. Everything happens more quickly.

Computers have two clocks. There's tick-really-fast clock that makes the hardware run. It doesn't tell the time. It just goes tick tick tick . . . really, really quickly. There's also a time-and-date clock, which is sometimes called a Real Time Clock or RTC. The Pi doesn't have a real RTC. It sets up a fake RTC — actually called the Fake RTC in the tech specs — when it boots by reading the time from the Internet. If there's no Internet, it loads the last time it remembers. This time is *always wrong.* So. Internet. Must be connected. Always.

But there's a catch. If you overclock your Pi too much, it melts — literally — and stops working. Before this destruction happens, your Pi can become less reliable. With less extreme overclocking it sometimes stops for no reason, but seems fine when you restart it.

To set up overclocking:

1. **Highlight the Overclock item in the Setup Options and press Enter.**

2. **Press Enter again to skip past the stern warning message.**

3. **Select your overclocking option.**

   There are five overclocking choices, as shown in Figure 4-9. The Medium option gives you enough of a speed boost to make a difference without being too dangerous.

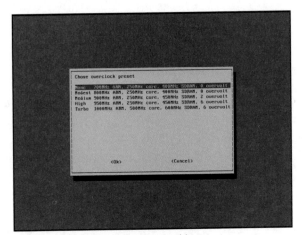

Figure 4-9: Setting up overclocking.

Don't select High and Turbo if you put your Pi in a case without good ventilation. Turbo especially needs a heat sink — like a radiator but smaller — stuck to the big chip on the Pi board. A small fan can help, too.

None is fine for basic use if you're not in a hurry. But the Pi is obviously slow for some jobs, like viewing web pages. Gentle overclocking can help with that.

Because the Pi is cheap, it's not the end of the world if you kill one. It's going to sting your pocket book, but the pain is much less than killing a Mac or PC. If you're fine with this, it's fine to experiment with overclocking.

Set up advanced options

Figure 4-10 shows the Advanced Options menu. To view it, select item 8 Advanced Options in the Setup Options menu. You can ignore most of the options, but a few may be useful:

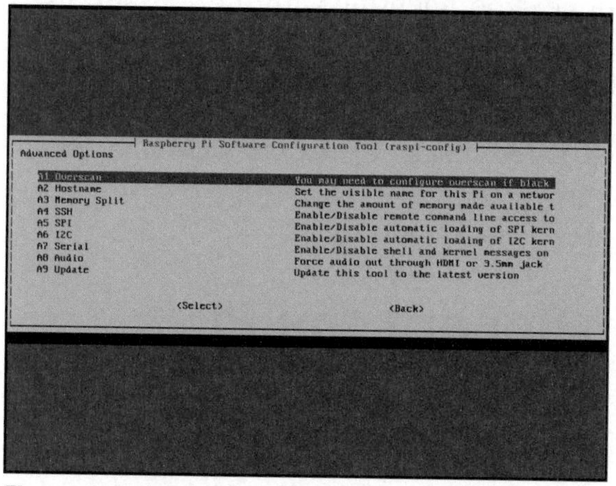

Figure 4-10: Looking at the Advanced options.

🖊 Change the overscan if the screen image is too big or small for your monitor — for example, if you see black bars around the image. There are no rules for this. Try different settings until you find one that works for you.

It's a good idea to disable (turn off) overscan. NOOBS gives the Pi display a black border, which is wasted space on most screens. Turning off overscan removes the border.

🗸 Change the hostname if you want to change the computer name to something other than raspberrypi. If you make the name a single letter, you get more space on the command line for commands. Or you can just ignore this setting.

🗸 Change the memory split if you want to use a screen with a bigger resolution, or you want to experiment with complicated games. You can push it up to 256 if you want to. The default setting works fine for simple games on a smaller monitor.

You can ignore the other settings. You only need to change them if you start connecting your Pi to special hardware. If you do, the manual for the hardware usually tells you what to change.

Finish with the setup options

When you're done experimenting with the settings, use the left/right arrow keys to select Finish and press Enter. If you changed anything important, your Pi reboots.

After it finishes, you're back at the command line, with the green rectangle prompt.

Shut Down or Reboot the Pi

This section is more important than it looks. In fact, it's very important, so don't ignore it or skip over it.

You can't turn off your Pi by pulling out the power plug or turning off the mains power.

Or rather you can, but you shouldn't — ever — except as a very last resort.

Linux does a lot of stuff as it works. In computer world, it throws its old clothes all over the room, leaves a pile of old plates on the desk, and generally makes a big mess.

You can't see this mess because it's on the memory card. But it's there. And it needs to be cleaned up regularly.

If you turn off the power, the mess stays. And it gets worse and worse every time you use your Pi.

But if you shut down or reboot the Pi, Linux cleans up the mess before going to sleep. It needs to be reminded to do this. The commands to make it happen are very simple.

To reboot your Pi, type the following command and press Enter:

```
sudo reboot
```

Your Pi cleans up the mess it made, shuts down, and restarts itself. When it's done, you'll see the command prompt.

To shut down your Pi when you've finished using it, type the following command and press Enter:

```
sudo poweroff
```

Your Pi cleans up the mess, but this time it shuts down and stays shut down. When the blinky light stops flashing on the Pi board and your monitor or TV goes blank, you can turn the power off.

The Pi board has a red power light. It stays on even after the board shuts down. Can you see any blinking or flickering after you power off? If not, the Pi has shut down, and you can turn off the power.

5

Use the Desktop

The easiest way to use your Pi is to open the built-in desktop. The Pi's desktop looks and works like other computer desktops. It's not exactly the same as a Windows or Mac desktop, but it's close enough. You don't have to learn a whole new way of using a computer.

Get Started with the Desktop

To make the desktop appear, type **startx** and press Enter when the dollar sign appears after you power up the Pi and log in with Pi as the username and "raspberry" as the password.

The Pi loads its desktop app — this takes a while — and eventually you see the screen shown in Figure 5-1. You can now click around with your mouse, open, drag, resize and close windows, launch apps, and do all the things you usually do on a desktop.

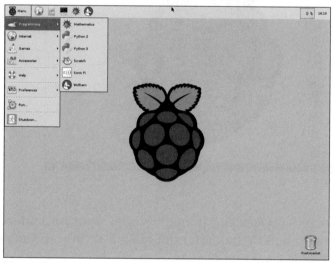

Figure 5-1

 On the Pi, the desktop is an application called LXDE, which is short for Lightweight X11 Desktop Environment. In theory, you can use a different desktop app. Two popular options are called Gnome and KDE. They have more features than LXDE and look different. Getting them to work on a Pi can be hard, so this book sticks with LXDE. It's already installed on the Pi, and it works just fine.

Use the Older Desktop

If you have an older version of the Pi software, you may see the screen shown in Figure 5-2. This is the old version of the desktop. It has all the same stuff, but some of it is in different places.

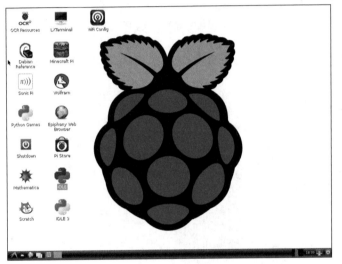

Figure 5-2

The old version is easier to understand. Icons for important apps like Scratch and Python are right in front of you. To launch the apps, double-click them.

In the new version, you can see the same things by clicking the menu at the top left. Scratch and Python are inside the Programming menu. To launch them, single-click them.

Don't sweat the differences. Both desktops have the same options. This book uses a mix of desktops so that you can get used to both. The desktop may change again in the future, so it's good to understand that sometimes things move around!

You might like the old desktop better. Unfortunately, you can't switch to the old desktop if your Pi software loads the new desktop. If you want the old desktop, you have to find and install an old version of NOOBS. And if you do that, you'll miss out on some cool updates.

Tour the Desktop

What does everything do? The desktop is split into two main areas.

- ✓ Taskbar

- ✓ Desktop area

Find the taskbar and desktop area

The *taskbar* is the area with the clock, the icons, the menu, and the graph thing with a percentage, which I explain in the upcoming section "Use the Activity Monitor."

On the old desktop, the taskbar is at the bottom of the screen. On the new desktop, it's at the top.

The old desktop has a few icons floating on it. On the new desktop, the background area has the Trashcan icon, and nothing else.

Work with windows

When you open a window, it floats over the desktop area. You can drag the window around, resize it, and do all the usual things to it.

To drag a window, click the colored area at the top with the name and/or description. It's called the *title bar* because it looks like a bar and it has a title.

You can click any window edge and drag it. You also can click a window bigger or smaller by clicking the bottom right corner.

The top right of the window has three small buttons. In order, they hide the window, make the window fill the screen, and close the window.

Sometimes closing a window quits an app. If an app has more than one window — some do, others don't — you need to use File⇨Quit to quit.

When you open a window, the desktop creates a tab in the taskbar. When you hide a window, the tab stays in the taskbar so that you can click it to show the window again.

Figure 5-3 shows a desktop with a handful of windows and tabs. All the windows are hidden, except one.

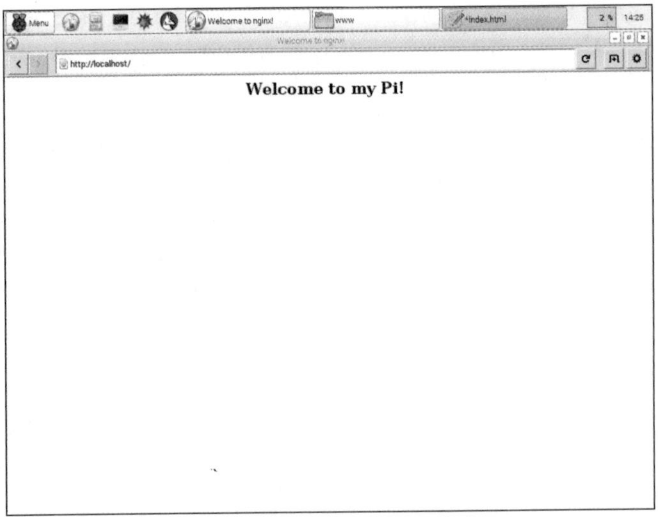

Figure 5-3

It's called a desktop because windows are supposed to work a bit like sheets of paper on a real wooden desk. Of course, you can't drag the corner of paper to make it bigger or smaller. And you can't run apps on paper. And you can't minimize paper to hide it. But apart from *that*, it's a bit like pushing paper on a real desk.

Use the Taskbar

Click on the Taskbar menu, and you can see submenus with all kinds of apps and features. If you've used the desktop on a Windows PC or a Mac, you can probably guess what some of them do.

The taskbar also has *quick launch* icons. They get special treatment. Icons in the desktop area are often hidden behind open windows, which makes them hard to use, but you can always see the quick launch icons.

Here's the list of quick launch icons for the new desktop:

✔ Epiphany Web Browser

✔ File Manager

✔ LXTerminal

✔ Mathematica

✔ Wolfram Language

This book doesn't have much to say about the last two items. They're for older Pi users who need help with high school and college math.

But you need to know how to use the first three items in the list to get the most value from the Pi's desktop.

Use the Quick Launch Icons

To use a Quick Launch app, click its icon. Your Pi launches the app, and its window appears on the desktop.

Desktop windows all work the same way.

Get started with Epiphany

Epiphany, shown in Figure 5-4, is the Pi's web browser. It works just like any other web browser. You can type a URL into the URL box and open multiple tabs. Figure 5-4 shows Epiphany with the main Google page loaded.

Figure 5-4

But it's not quite like other browsers, and there are a couple of things you need to know about it.

✔ It has a strange name.

✔ It's reallllly slow.

The first thing isn't a big deal. The weird name means sudden realization. It's really just an excuse to give the Pi a web browser with a name that has pi in it.

The second thing is more important. The Pi is not a fast computer, and Epiphany is not a fast web browser. It can take a minute or two for some pages to load. Epiphany also has problems loading some pages. If you see an error message when you try to load a page, it's not usually your fault.

It's fine to use Epiphany to test a web server on your Pi. So if you need to look things up online, it's best to use a browser on another computer. Otherwise, you'll be waiting for it to finish loading pages — a lot!

Using other browsers

The Pi has another browser called NetSurf hidden away in the preinstalled applications. It's quite a bit faster than Epiphany — it's almost fast enough to be usable — but it's not so good at getting the layout of web pages right, so words are often smushed up into other words.

Even so, it's worth loading NetSurf to see how you like it. It's hidden in a special folder, so you can't launch it from the desktop. You can find out more about that special folder later in this chapter — including instructions for finding it.

You can't use the most popular browsers, like Chrome, Firefox, or Internet Explorer, on the Pi. You can install a special version of Chrome called Chromium, but you can't install it from the desktop. When you know more about Linux commands you can try searching the web for Install Chromium on Pi for instructions. Chapters 8 and 10 explain how to use text commands to install software.

In Epiphany, you can search the web for a word or phrase by typing it into the URL box and pressing Enter. Epiphany uses a search engine called Duck Go. It gives similar results to Google, but includes bigger ads. If you want to use Google instead, you can open the main Google page (www.google.com) and search from there.

Explore files with File Manager

Files are the information you store on your computers. To keep files organized, they're often kept in *folders*. Folders can contain more folders. Or more files. Or both. (But they can't contain squirrels. Which is a good thing.)

To help you find your way around, the Pi includes a file manager app called File Manager.

You can find the icon to the right of the web browser icon in the taskbar. It looks like a battered filing cabinet. To launch File Manager, click the icon. Figure 5-5 shows the file list that appears.

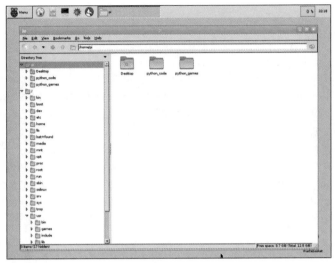

Figure 5-5

Understand files in File Manager

File Manager shows a list of folders at the left of the window. To see the files inside a folder, click it. The files appear in the right of the window.

To see the folders inside a folder, click the tiny triangle next to the folder name. When a folder is *open* — showing the folders inside it — the triangle points down. When a folder is closed, the triangle points to the right, at the folder name.

The complete list of folders is called the *directory tree* because it's a bit like an upside-down tree. The tree builds down from a root, which is the super-important everything-starts-here folder.

This folder is so important it has a super-important name. It's called / — a single backslash.

Maybe / is easier to type than `thisisthesuperimportant` `rootfolder`.

If you refer to Figure 5-5, you can see that the `superimportant-` `rootfolder` includes a lot of other folders. They hold the files and folders that make your Pi work.

You can also see a folder called `pi` at the top of the list. This is your home folder. Every user on a Pi has a home folder. Because you spend a lot of time at home, File Manager includes it in the directory tree so that you can get to it quickly without having to find it in the main tree.

Does this mean it's in two places? No! There's only one home folder. But you can get to it in two ways in File Manager. One way is a quick-click to save you having to take the long way. The other way is the long way. It takes a lot of scrolling and clicking, so it's *very* handy to have a shortcut.

Move around in File Manager

The directory tree gives every single file in your Pi its own address — which is just the list of folders you need to click through to get to the file.

Addresses look like this:

```
/home/pi/mystuff/and_so_on...
```

File addresses are also called *paths*. Getting to an address is a bit like walking down a path with lots of side alleys and turnings.

To get to a file at that address:

1. **Click the `/home` folder.**

2. **Click the `/pi` folder inside home.**

3. **Keep clicking folders to look inside them until you get to the folder you want.**

As you open more and more folders, File Manager always shows you where you are. It's hard to get lost.

Here's a real example, which takes you to the pre-installed apps in your Pi, including the web browsers mentioned in the sidebar "Using other web browsers":

```
/usr/share/raspi-ui-overrides/applications
```

See whether you can click your way through the address to find the files. You'll need to scroll down through the tree to see all the folders in /usr/share because there's a lot of stuff in there.

Figure 5-6 shows all the apps in File Manager. The folder includes the apps in the desktop menus and some others. You can double-click any of them to launch them.

Figure 5-6

While you're in this folder, you may want to try setting up WiFi with the WiFiConfiguration app. Double-click it to launch it.

The Pi isn't great at WiFi. For example, it doesn't scan for networks automatically. The best way to find full instructions is to search online for WiFi Pi setup.

Meet god-mode

You'll soon discover that the Pi doesn't let you look inside certain files and folders. In fact, you're locked out of most of the file system!

There is a reason for this. The Pi's Linux operating system locks you out deliberately so that you can't break something by accident. As an ordinary user, you're not allowed to touch the Pi's moving parts or stick your finger into any power sockets.

Frustrating, huh? It would be even more frustrating if you were locked out forever. But there is a back door. If you know the magic words, you can promote yourself to a special god-user called `root` and gain superpowers that let you do whatever you want.

Chapter 10 has more about becoming the god-user. You don't need to worry about it for now. You only need god-mode if you're installing new software or changing something important in your Pi.

Mac and Windows computers include god-mode, too. They just hide it better. When your Mac or PC asks for your password before it does something — that's a god-mode check.

Use the Activity Monitor

Your Pi often needs to think for a while when you ask it to do something. Windows computers show you an hourglass while they're thinking. Mac computers show a spinning colored wheel, which is sometimes called the pizza wheel even though no one has ever seen a pizza with all those colors.

The Pi has the Activity Monitor. It's the box with a scrolling graph and a percentage at the right of the taskbar.

The Activity Monitor is more important than it looks because it shows you how hard your Pi is working. At 0 percent your Pi is doing nothing. At 100 percent, your Pi is working very hard. If you ask it to do something when it's working very hard, it's going to take longer than usual to do it.

There's a clock to the right of the Activity Monitor. When your Pi is connected to the Internet, the clock sets itself. If you click the clock, you can see a calendar.

Use the Desktop Menu

The Desktop menu includes a selection of useful apps. To open the menu, click the Menu button at the top left of the taskbar.

On the old desktop, click the spiky shape (it's the logo for the desktop, but you'd never guess) at the bottom left.

You can drag the mouse over the menu items to see more items in each group. Click an app to launch it.

Figure 5-7 shows the Accessories.

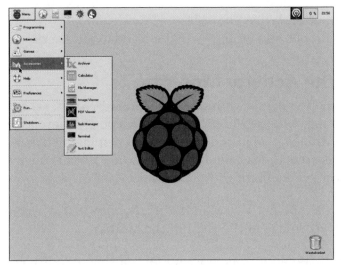

Figure 5-7

Edit Files

The desktop includes an editor. You can make a small change to the Pi to make it easier to use on a network.

To edit a file using the Leaf text editor, start by clicking the taskbar Menu button and drag the mouse over the Accessories item. Move it to the right and down a bit and click the big green leaf icon labeled Text Editor.

The text editor loads with a blank window. You can type text into the window with your keyboard, edit the text with your keyboard and mouse, and choose File ⇨ Save As to save the file.

You can also load an existing file by choosing File⇨Open. The editor displays a file selector.

The selector works a bit like a smaller version of File Manager. It has a list of folders and shortcuts at the left and a window showing the files in each location at the right.

But it doesn't show the super-important folder named /. Instead, it has a shortcut labeled File System, — which takes you to / because / *is* the file system.

Double-click File System and work your way through the folders to

```
/etc/network
```

Double-click the file named interfaces, as shown in Figure 5-8. You can also click the file once and then click the Open button.

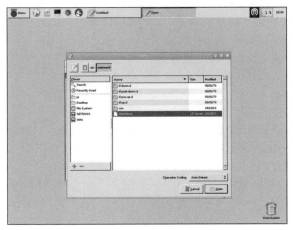

Figure 5-8

See those buttons above the folder and file area? Every time you double-click a folder to open it, the file selector adds it as a button. The buttons are a super-speedy shortcut feature. Click a button to go straight to that folder. You'll also see a Recently Opened list in the file area. The file selector remembers the files you worked on recently, so you don't have to find them again — you can double-click the name of the file instead.

The editor loads the file. You'll see some cryptic computer gobbledeegook, as shown in Figure 5-9. The gobbledeegook is a collection of magic words. They tell your Pi how to connect to the local network and the Internet.

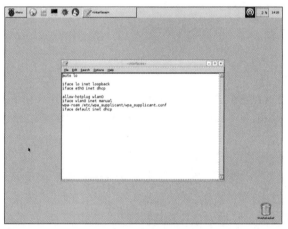

Figure 5-9

If you know the right magic words, you can edit the file to make your Pi work differently.

Linux is more hands-on than Windows or OS X, and a lot of important settings are hidden in text files.

How do you know which file to edit, and how to change it? You don't. Linux is complicated. You will never, ever be able to guess how to find most of its settings or how to change them after you find them.

You have to look them up online. Whenever you want to change a setting in your Pi, search online for instructions.

This isn't cheating! Professional developers do it all the time when they don't know how to do something. It's not as neat and easy as changing a few settings in a preferences panel. But once you figure out how to do it, you can customize your Pi and make it do things you can't do with other computers.

Week 2
Simple Programming Projects

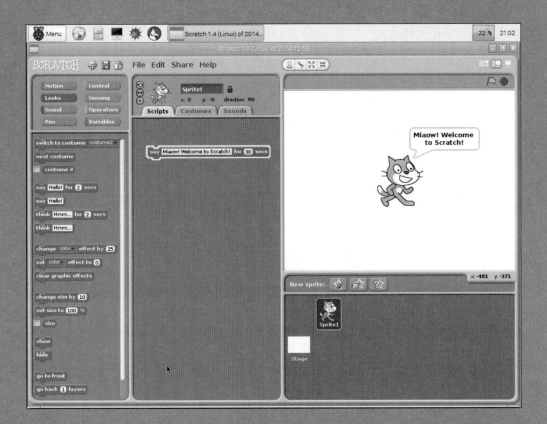

In this part, you'll . . .

See the bonus chapters on getting deeper into Scratch and making music with Sonic Pi at www.dummies.com/extras/raspberrypiforkids.

Start Scratch from Scratch

You can use your Pi to make games and play with real code. This project is about a simple way to get started with coding. It's called Scratch, and it's a lot of fun.

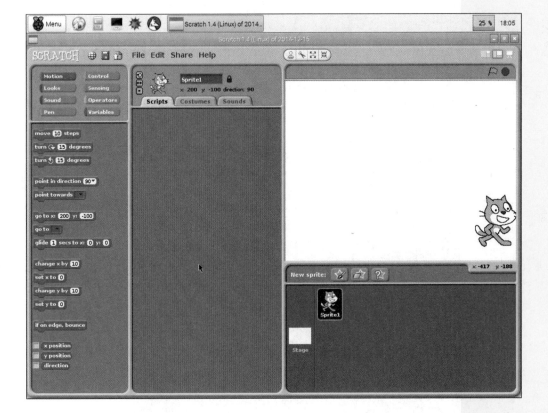

Understand Scratch

Scratch is the simplest way ever to make your own software by creating computer code. Usually when you write code, you type words that look a bit — but not much — like English.

With Scratch you don't have to type anything. You get a big (virtual) box of blocks and a *stage* where things happen. The stage has characters called *sprites,* which can move around the stage, bump off the walls and off each other, and do all kinds of other stuff.

Each block does something different. Some blocks move a sprite. Other blocks turn a sprite or make it change color. Some blocks check whether a sprite is touching another sprite or the sides of the stage.

You can make sprites show talk bubbles or think bubbles, get bigger or smaller, or change them in many other ways. Figure 6-1 shows a sprite saying something with a talk bubble.

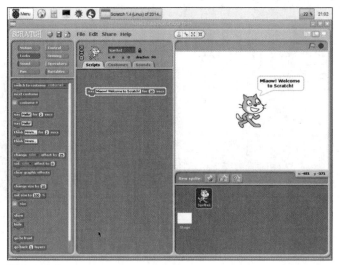

Figure 6-1

Scratch was made for kids, but adults can use it, too. Scratch is a really good way to get started with coding before moving to more complicated computer languages like Python.

A *computer language* is a way to tell a computer what you want it to do. There are lots and lots of computer languages. They're all different, but a lot of languages do the same kind of stuff but use different words for it — a bit like French and English. Scratch is a very simple language that gives you a lot of ready-made words to use, so you don't have to work hard to learn them and remember them.

Connect Blocks and Making Scripts

To make a game or tell a story, drag the blocks into a list with your mouse. The blocks clip together on the screen, a bit like real plastic blocks.

Lists are called *scripts*. When you click on a script, Scratch goes through the blocks one by one, and each block does something to the sprites it controls.

The blocks move, change, spin, or check a sprite in the order you set. Special blocks can repeat some or all of a script over and over or a set number of times. You can also make your script remember numbers and sentences and do simple math.

You can have more than one sprite on the stage at a time. You can also set the stage background to make your story or game look more exciting.

You don't have to use Scratch on your Pi. The scratch website at `http://scratch.mit.edu` includes a version of Scratch that runs in a web browser. The Pi version is less polished than the web version. But you probably have the Pi all to yourself, so you won't have to wait to use the family computer to use Scratch.

Find and Start Scratch

You can start Scratch only when the Pi's desktop is open. Here's what you need to do:

1. **If you've just booted your Pi and you're at the command prompt, type** startx **and press Enter.**

Figure 6-2 shows you where to find Scratch.

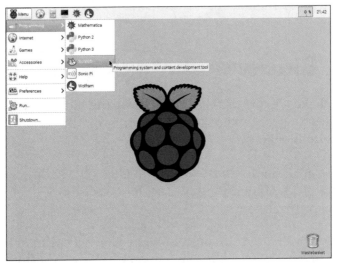

Figure 6-2

2. **When the desktop appears, click the Menu button at the top left of the screen.**

3. **Move the mouse down to Programming.**

4. **When the next menu slides out, move the mouse to Scratch and click on the Scratch item.**

After a while, the Scratch window appears.

You may not see the same options on your Pi, or they may be in different places. Look for the words Programming and Scratch in the menu system to find them.

Look around Scratch

The Scratch window looks like it has a lot going on, but it's not as complicated as it looks.

From left to right, look for four boxes:

✔ **Block box:** This box has a list of all the blocks you can use. Blocks come in different colors, and the box shows only one color at a time.

✔ **Scripts/Costumes/Sounds box:** This box is where you clip blocks together to make scripts. You can also make new costumes — sprite shapes — and work with sounds by clicking the tags near the top of the box.

✔ **Stage box:** The big white area with the cat is the stage. This box is where you play your game or tell your story.

✔ **Sprite box:** The area under the stage shows all the sprites in your story or game.

When you start Scratch, it makes a sprite for you. The sprite looks like a cartoon cat. You can change the way the sprite looks by changing its costume. You can make it move by changing its position on the stage.

Understand the Stage

The stage doesn't understand up, down, left, or right.

Instead, it uses a system with two magic numbers, so you can just tell a sprite to move to the right by some distance. The numbers have special names: x and y. The x number sets the left/right position. The y number sets the up/down position.

x and y are sometimes called *coordinates,* which is a big, complicated mathy word for "this is how we use two numbers to work out where something is."

When x and y are both 0, the sprite is dead center of the stage. To move a sprite right, set x to more than 0. To move it left, set x to less than 0.

The size of x tells you how far away the sprite is from the middle of the stage. The sign (minus or nothing) tells you whether it's left or right of the middle.

So when x is 100, the sprite is in the right half of the stage. When it's x is –100, it's in the left half of the stage.

Up and down work the same way. When y is 100, the sprite is in the top half. When y is –100, it's in the bottom half.

x and y are completely separate. They're independent, so you can move the sprite left or right without changing how far up/down it is. And you can move it up and down without changing its left/right position.

To move it up and down *and* left and right, you have to change x and y together.

Table 6-1 has a cheat sheet.

Why does Scratch work like this? Wouldn't it be easier to say left, right, up, and down? It might be, but this x y idea is how it's done in math and in grown-up game and app programming, so Scratch copies how they work.

Table 6-1	Moving on the Stage with x and y
How Big Are x and y?	**Where Is the Sprite?**
x doesn't have a minus sign (100)	Right half of the stage
x has a minus sign (–100)	Left half of the stage
y doesn't have a minus sign (75)	Top half of the stage
x has a minus sign (–75)	Bottom half of the stage
x is zero (0)	Dead center left/right only
y is zero (0)	Dead center up/down only
x and y are zero (0)	Dead center left/right and up/down

Move a Sprite with go to

You can also move a sprite using go to:

1. **If you can't see the blue blocks in the block list, click the blue Motion button near the top left of the screen.**

2. **Look down the list to find the block called go to x: y:.**

   When you click it or include it in a script, it sets the *x* and *y* numbers that move a sprite. If you haven't changed anything, the numbers are both 0, so the block looks like this:

   ```
   go to x:0 y:0
   ```

   You can see the *x* and *y* numbers in the block.

3. **Double-click the x: number, and when it turns gray, type 200 and press Enter.**

   With a new *x* number, the sprite jumps toward the right of the screen. Cool! See how it works?

4. **Now double-click the y: number, and when it turns gray, type –100.**

   The sprite moves down. Figure 6-3 shows where it ends up.

 Your sprite may not be in the same place. The width and height of the stage depend on the width and height of your screen (monitor), so your stage may not be the same width and height as the stage in the image. You don't need to worry about where the sprite is, as long as it moves!

Center a sprite

Can you work out how to use a go to block to move a sprite to the middle of the stage? Table 1-1, earlier in the project, offers a clue.

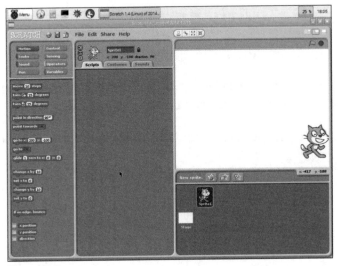

Figure 6-3

You can probably guess that if you change *x* and *y* to 0, the sprite will jump back to the middle.

Now you can play with typing other numbers into the *x* and *y* boxes to see what they do. After a while, you should be able to guess what a number does before you try it.

If you look at the block list, you can see other blocks you can use now. Click once on the following to see what they do:

```
change x by [number]
set x to [number]
change y by [number]
set y to [number]
```

Glide a sprite

People and things in the real world don't usually jump instantly from one place to another. To make movement look more realistic, you can use the glide block.

The glide block works like the go to block, but it has an extra number, which sets how long it takes the sprite to glide from one place to another.

Try changing the *x* and *y* numbers and the time in seconds in the glide block to see what it does.

Move and turn a sprite

Scratch gives you another way to move sprites. Instead of moving to somewhere on the stage, you can tell a sprite to move in the direction it's facing. You can also turn it to make it face in a different direction.

Use the move, turn, and point blocks to move like this. They're at the top of the block list. Try clicking on them and changing the numbers in them to see what they do.

There's also a point in direction block that makes the sprite turn to face the direction you set. The direction is set in degrees, which are like small turning steps. So 360 degrees turns the sprite all the way around, which is kind of pointless. And 180 degrees turns it halfway around, while 90 degrees turns it a quarter of the way around.

You can click the number box to set your own number, or you can select four directions from a menu. See whether you can work out which numbers mean left, right, up, and down.

Understand turn and rotation

If you turn a sprite, it may not turn on the stage, even though it's pointing in a new direction. This may be confusing, because although the sprite has turned because you told it to, it still looks like it's facing that way!

The complicated mathy word for turning something is *rotation*. Scratch gives you a choice about how the sprite looks when you rotate it.

If you look closely, you can find three tiny buttons to the left of the sprite in the top part of the middle window.

You can click any button to select it. From top to bottom, they work like this:

- **can rotate:** Click this button to make sure the sprite always turns. It can face up, down, left, right, or any direction in between. Sometimes this means it's upside down.

- **only face left/right:** The sprite faces only left or right, even if it's pointing up or down. It's never upside down.

- **don't rotate:** The sprite always faces the same way. You can still change its direction, but you only ever see one direction on the stage.

Make a Simple Script

You can make a simple script by dragging blocks to the Scripts area in the middle of the screen:

1. **Drag a move block to the Scripts area.**

2. **Drag a turn block to the Scripts area and hold it just under the move block without lifting your finger from the mouse button.**

   Scratch shows a wide white line, like the one in Figure 6-4.

3. **Let go of the mouse.**

   When you let go of the mouse button, the bottom block clips to the top block.

   You made a script!

When you click anywhere on the script, Scratch steps through each block in turn. This script makes the sprite move, and then it makes it turn.

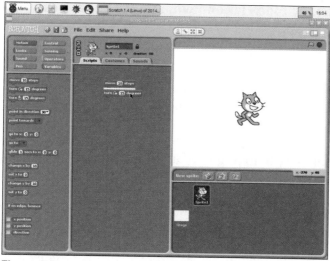

Figure 6-4

This script has only two blocks, but if you made a script with hundreds of blocks, Scratch would start at the top block, do what it says, move to the next block, do what it says, and so on, all the way down the list, in order.

Making a script work is called *running* a script. Imagine a script wizard running from the top of the script to the bottom and making each block work in turn. Scripts work a lot like that, only you can't see the wizard because he's hiding behind the stage.

You can clip blocks to the top of a script as well as the bottom. You can clip a block whenever it has a slot or a tag.

Break up a script

Sometimes you want to break a script. Maybe you want to take off the last few blocks. Or maybe you want to make a gap in the middle so that you can put more blocks in.

To break a script:

1. **Click on a block and drag it.**

    The script splits, and Scratch shows the white line.

2. **Drag the block far enough, and the white box vanishes.**

Now you have two blocks, or maybe two smaller scripts.

Right-click on blocks

Scratch has some cool extra tools. To see them, right-click on a block or a script.

- **help:** Click help to get a hint about what a block does. The hint appears in a window. Click OK to make the window go away.

- **duplicate:** Click duplicate to make a copy of a script or block. The copy appears in the Scripts area.

- **delete:** Click delete to get rid of a script or block from the script area. The block or script disappears. If you do this by accident and change your mind, choose Edit⇨Undelete from the menu at the top of the Scratch window to make the script/block reappear.

Make a reset script for a sprite

Can you work out how to make a reset script for a sprite now? Say that you want to join two blocks to move the sprite to x:0 and y:0 and turn it so that it faces to the right.

Try clipping blocks together and changing the numbers inside them until you've made a script that does this. Remember, you can have more than one script in the Scripts area at a time, so you can leave this script lying around, if you want.

Control a Script

Sometimes you want a script to do something over and over. If you broke up the script in the previous section, put it back together. Click on it a few times. The sprite moves and turns each time.

You can make a script do the same thing over and over by clicking it over and over. That works fine for a few repeats, but what if you want to repeat something hundreds of times?

You could use the duplicate right-click tool to make lots and lots of copies of your simple script and clip them together to make one big script.

That works for maybe ten repeats, but it's a boring way to make a script do something hundreds of times.

Scratch has a better way. Click the Control button at the top of the block library. It has an orange edge. When you click, it you see a new set of blocks.

These are control blocks. They make your scripts smarter.

You can use control blocks do things like

- **Repeat some blocks forever.**

- **Repeat some blocks as many times as you want, then carry on.**

- **Start a script when you press a key.**

- **Make a script wait for a while.**

- **Make a script wait until something happens.**

- **Repeat a script until something happens.**

- **Check and test numbers, sprite positions, and other things.**

- **Stop a script.**

- **Stop all scripts.**

Use control blocks

Control blocks go in three places:

- ✔ **At the start of a script**

- ✔ **At the end of a script**

- ✔ **Around other blocks**

Start control blocks have a round top. You can't clip a block on top of them. They have to go first because they wait for something to happen. The script can't start until it happens!

For example, the when [space] key pressed block starts a script when you press the space key. You can pick a different key using the menu in the block.

End control blocks have a flat bottom. You can't clip a block under them. They have to go at the end of a script because they tell the script to stop.

Around scripts have a space inside them. They look a bit like fat hairclips. To use them, drag them around the script you want to control.

You may have to split the script to pull out the blocks you want to control first and then glue it back together after you added the around block.

You can try out the repeat block. Drag it from the block list to the script area and clip it around the two blocks there already. The bottom end of the clip stretches to fit around the blocks.

Figure 6-5 shows the result. Click the block, and the sprite moves and turns. It repeats ten times unless you change the number by clicking it and typing in a new number.

If it doesn't turn, check which rotation button is lit. For details, see the section "Move and turn a sprite," earlier in this project.

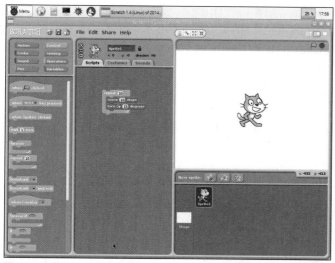

Figure 6-5

Stop scripts

Click the number in the `repeat` block and type **100** and press Enter. Click the script again.

Now the sprite moves and turns over and over. It keeps moving for a long time.

Did you get bored? If you want to stop a script early, you can click the red button above the stage. The green flag next to it lights up when a script is running.

You can also click a script to stop it. While it's running you can see a white border around it. When you stop it, the border disappears.

Make a Simple Bounce Script

Can you make a script that bounces the sprite off the edges of the screen? There's an easy way to do this, and a hard way.

The easy way is to use the `if on edge, bounce` block in the Motion block list. Clip a `move` block and the `if on edge, bounce` block together. Put them inside a `forever` control block.

If you worked out how to make a reset script, click it to move the sprite to the middle of the screen.

Figure 6-6 shows you how to clip the blocks together.

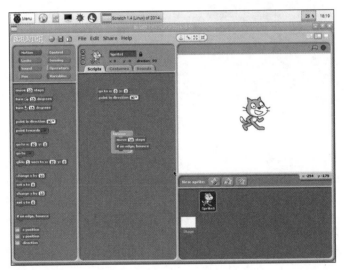

Figure 6-6

Optionally, you can click the middle only face left-right rotation button to keep the sprite the right way up when it bounces.

Click the script. The sprite should bounce between the two sides of the stage! Click the script again to stop it.

What happens if you turn the sprite first? Click a turn block to turn the sprite. If you don't have the can rotate button selected, you won't see any difference. But click the script to run it again.

The sprite bounces up and down and left and right! Click the script to stop it.

Introduce Variables

What does bounce do? What happens when the sprite bounces?

If you think about it, a bounce means it turns to face the other way, so you could use a turn block to make it bounce. You could tell the sprite to face left when it bounces off the right edge of the screen and face right when it bounces off the left edge.

But maybe you want to make the sprite do something else — like jump when you press one key, hide behind another sprite when you press a different key, or bounce before it hits the edge.

To do that, you need to know where it is. And you have to be able to change where it is.

You could make a lot of go to blocks with a different *x* and *y* for every place on the stage the sprite might be. But that would be a *lot* of blocks.

A better way would be to remember and change *x* and *y* positions as it needs to. You can do this in Scratch using variable blocks.

A *variable* is like a box that holds a number. The box has a name, so you can tell it from other boxes. And it has space for a number.

Variables can remember letters, words, and sentences, too.

Use variables

Scratch can do three clever things with variables. The first is make them. Variables have special blocks, and when you make one variable, you get some special blocks to help you use it. You can set the variable to a number or add a number to it.

When you make a variable, it appears on the stage. You don't always want this, so you can use a hide variable block to make it go away. And you can use a show variable block to make it come back.

The second clever thing is math. You can add, subtract, multiply, and divide variables by some number. You can even add, subtract, multiply, and divide one variable by another!

The final clever thing is best of all. You can use a variable wherever you see a number. For example, you can tell a go to block to use a variable you make. When you click the go to block or when Scratch reaches it in a script, the block moves the sprite to the number stored in the variable.

This gives you way more options than moving a sprite to the same place all the time. You can change the numbers by hand. Or with math. Or by making them follow other numbers, like the position of some other sprite.

Make a variable

To make a variable, click the darker orange Variables button at the bottom right of the block types in the block list area. Three buttons appear. You can click them to

- ✔ **Make a variable**

- ✔ **Delete a variable**

- ✔ **Make a list**

A *list* is a special kind of a variable that holds other variables. It's like a big box with lots of smaller boxes inside it. They're numbered so that you can tell them apart and do things like get the third box and change what's inside it. You can ignore lists for now.

To make a new variable

1. **Click the make a variable pattern.**

   You see a window like the one in Figure 6-7.

2. **Type** sprite1_x **into the Variable Name? box.**

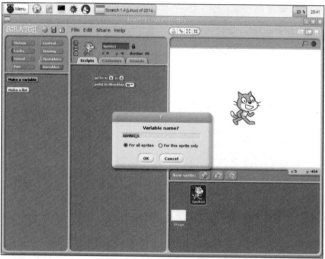

Figure 6-7

3. **Leave the For All Sprites option checked and click OK.**

   Whoa! Stuff happens! Scratch makes some new blocks. And if you look at the stage, you'll see a box appears, with the name of your variable sprite1_x and a number.

When you make a new variable, the number is always 0 because you haven't changed it yet. Figure 6-8 shows what you get.

Can you use variables to replace any number? You totally can! You can use a `set` block to set a variable to the value of another variable. In a `change` block, you can make the by value a variable. You can make scripts that are really smart, with variables passing values to other variables between sprites all over the stage. There are almost no limits to what you can do.

Understand For All Sprites and This Sprite Only

When you make a variable, you can tell Scratch to make it *private* for each sprite by clicking the For This Sprite Only option. If it's private, other sprites can't read it, change, or even see it.

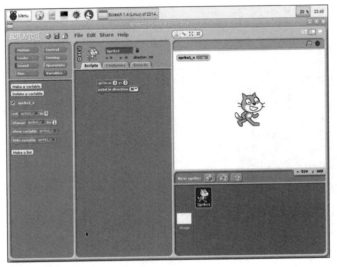

Figure 6-8

Sometimes privacy is a good thing. It means you can use the same variable names in different sprites, so you can copy a script and use it with a new sprite without changing anything.

But sometimes you want one sprite to know what's happening in the scripts for another sprite. That's when you leave For All Sprites selected as you make the variable. Now you can use the variable in every script for every sprite.

This choice looks like something you can ignore, but it's a big deal. Programmers spend a lot of time thinking about whether to make variables private or public. If you make everything public, you can make a big mess and never be sure which script is changing which variable. If you have too many private variables you can't get at the variables you need.

Plug variables into blocks

The big deal about variables is that you can use them to replace numbers. Instead of a fixed number like 10, which never changes, you can use a variable that you control with the power of control blocks and math.

Scratch does some clever tricks to make this work. You can literally drag and drop a variable on top of a number to replace it:

1. **Drag your sprite1_x variable block and drop it into the Scripts area.**

   Ignore the set, change, show, and hide blocks. You want the block with the variable name and nothing else.

2. **Click the Motion block type at the top left of the block list window and drag a go to block onto the script window.**

3. **And for your next trick, drag the variable block and drop it on the white number box.**

   If you do it right, the variable replaces the 0 that used to be there. Your new block should look like the one in Figure 6-9.

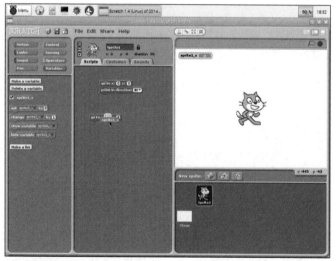

Figure 6-9

Set and change the variable value

The number inside the variable is called the *value.* Click the Variables button at the top of the block list and find the set and change blocks.

When you click a set block or use it in a script, it sets the value to the number in the block.

When you click a change block or use it in a script, it adds the number after the value. When you start, that number is 1, so the block adds 1 to a value. But you can click it and change it.

Try it now:

1. **Click the number in the set block and change it to, say, 10.**

2. **Click the set block and watch what happens.**

3. **Click the change block a few times.**

   Did you see what happened? The sprite1_x value box on the stage changed when you clicked the blocks. Figure 6-10 shows the changes.

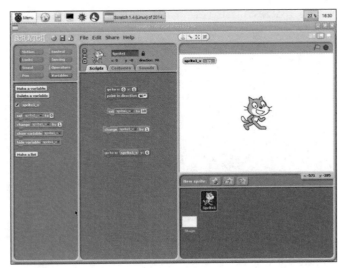

Figure 6-10

The set and change blocks are in the Scripts area so you can see them more clearly. You don't need to copy them to use them. You can click them and change the numbers inside them in the block list. But often if you're playing with blocks, it's good to make a copy in the Scripts area so that you can change them and maybe plug them into a script when you're done.

Understand variables in blocks

Something didn't happen — the sprite didn't move. Why not?

The go to block moves the sprite only when you click on it or when Scratch runs it as part of a script. It doesn't move the sprite when you change a variable inside it.

You might think it would, but it doesn't — for a good reason.

You want to be able to change a value without lots of stuff happening as a result. Scratch works better if it does only the stuff you tell it to, not if it does stuff because it thinks you might want it.

So if you want a sprite to move, you have to set a variable in go to block and then click the block or run it inside a script. Otherwise, no movement.

Other blocks work the same way. They read the variable value only when you click on them, or Scratch reaches them when it's running a script.

Show and hide variables

What do you think happens if you click on the show variable and hide variable blocks? Try it now!

Were you surprised? hide variable hides the value box on the stage. show variable makes it appear on the stage.

You can use these blocks to clean up the stage when you have so many variables it looks like a mess. You don't usually need to look at all the values at once. Sometimes you don't need to look at the values at all — which is when you need these blocks.

Meet Sonic Pi

Sonic Pi is a free music synthesizer and sequencer. You don't play it from a keyboard or other instrument — you play it by writing code.

If you're not into music, it's a cool way to make some weird sounds. And if you are into music, the only limit is your imagination!

Unlike Python, which is used for all kinds of projects, the Sonic Pi computer language is used only by Sonic Pi. You can't write Sonic Pi code to draw pictures, make games, or run a website! Some of the things Sonic Pi can do appear in other computer languages, too. But the code that makes them happen doesn't look the same.

Get Started with Sonic Pi

If the desktop isn't already running, launch it with the startx command.

Click the menu button at the top left and choose Programming ➪ Sonic Pi, as shown in Figure 7-1.

Figure 7-1

Sonic Pi takes a while to load. When the splash screen with the logo and the information about Sonic Pi disappears, click the second button at the top right of the window bar to maximize the window and make it fill the screen.

You can also close the About window with the credits. You don't need it while Sonic Pi is running.

Set Up Sound on the Pi

Sound on the Pi just works — mostly. You may need to experiment with the Sonic Pi settings — called Prefs or Preferences — depending on the hardware you use to listen to the sound.

To show the Prefs, click the tiny arrows at the far right of the bar with the buttons at the top of the window. The arrows are next to the Help button.

When a button labeled Prefs appears, click it.

Figure 7-2 shows the Preferences. You can use Raspberry Pi System Volume Slider to set the volume.

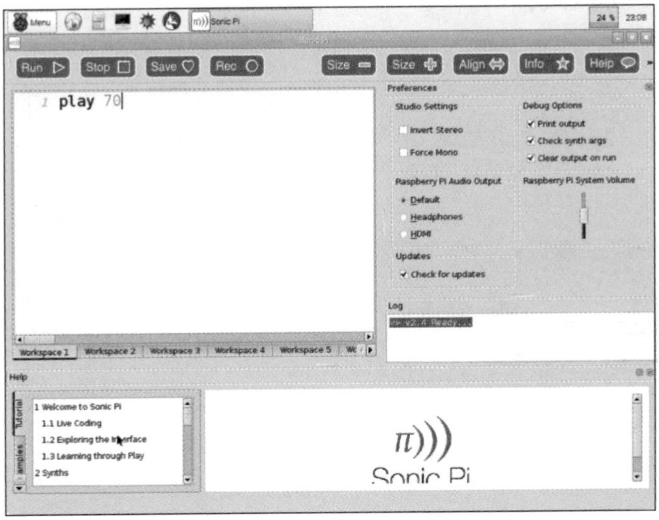

Figure 7-2

 The sound quality of the Pi's headphone socket isn't brilliant. And because the Pi is a slow computer, you can't make really big, fat, complicated sounds with it. But you can still have a lot of fun playing with note patterns, synths, samples, and FX — even if you don't know much about music, or have never tried to play an instrument.

 The Pi 2 is much better for music than the original Pi. It's faster, so you can make bigger sounds. You can also buy external sound boards for your Pi with much better sound quality. Search online for Pi sound card for details.

If you don't hear any sound when you use Sonic Pi, you probably need to select a different item in the Raspberry Pi Audio Output box.

If you have a TV or monitor connected but you want to listen through the Pi's headphone socket, click the Headphones item.

If you want to listen to the sound through your TV or monitor speakers, click the HDMI button.

If you leave the setting unchanged, the Pi guesses what you want. If you have a screen connected with an HDMI lead and it doesn't have speakers, you may not hear anything unless you change the Prefs to send the sound to the headphones.

Click the tiny cross at the top right of the Prefs when you've finished.

 The Pi has a very basic sound chip, and the sound on the Model B+/A+ isn't great. It's better on the Pi 2. The easy way to hear sound is to plug some headphones or earbuds into the socket on the side of the Pi. If you have some speakers, you can plug them in to the same socket. Keep the volume down at first! Turn it up to a comfortable level using the Prefs so that you don't deafen yourself.

Play Tunes with Sonic Pi

Before the guided tour of Sonic Pi, later in this project, you can make some simple music. Figure 7-3 shows an example.

To make music, follow these steps:

1. **Launch Sonic Pi.**

   When you launch Sonic Pi, you see a single command in the code window:

   ```
   play 70
   ```

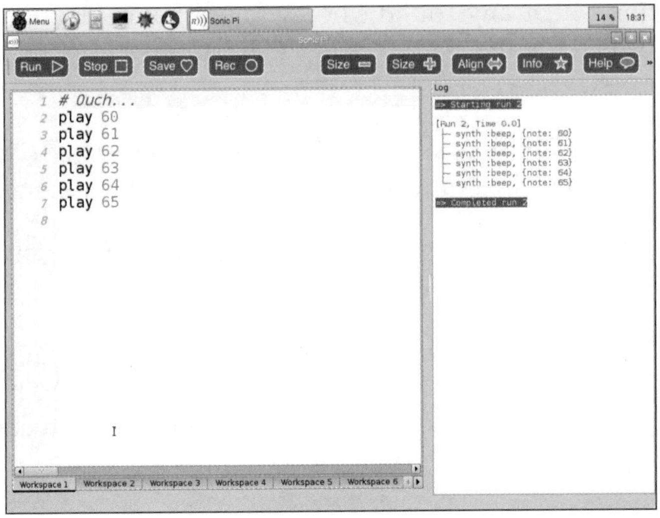

Figure 7-3

2. **Click the Run button at the top left.**

   Did you hear a note?

3. **If you didn't hear anything, go back to the Prefs and experiment with the settings until clicking Run makes a noise.**

4. **If you do hear a note, click in the code window and press the Backspace key a couple of times to delete 70.**

5. **Now type 60 instead so that the code looks like this:**

   ```
   play 60
   ```

6. **Click Run again.**

   Can you hear how the note changed? The sound — the pitch — is lower.

   You can play notes together.

7. **Edit the code so that it looks like the following and click Run:**

   ```
   play 60
   play 64
   play 67
   ```

   Those notes make a nice sound.

8. **Edit the code so that it looks like this and click Run again:**

   ```
   play 60
   play 61
   play 62
   play 63
   play 64
   play 65
   ```

   That's not such a nice sound, is it?

Musicians know which notes sound good together, and which notes don't. Music that sounds nice all the time is boring, so most music has a mix of nice and not-so-nice sounds and notes.

Play with time

You don't have to play all the notes at the same time. You can tell Sonic Pi to sleep between notes to make a gap, like this:

```
play 60
sleep 1
play 64
sleep 1
play 67
```

Sonic Pi reads the 1 as 1 whole beat. Most music uses shorter notes. You usually divide beats into half-beats, quarter-beats, and eighth-beats. For very fast music, you can use sixteenths or even thirty-seconds.

Because Sonic Pi was made by programmers and not musicians, you have to give it a beat fraction as a decimal number. Table 7-1 is a cheat sheet for beat counting.

Table 7-1	Neat Beat Cheat Sheet
Beat Fraction	**Sleep Time**
1	1
Half	0.5
Quarter	0.25
Eighth	0.125
Sixteenth	0.0625
Thirty-second	0.03125

Try the following:

```
play 60
sleep 0.125
play 64
sleep 0.5
play 67
sleep 0.25
play 64
sleep 0.125
play 60
```

Using different beats creates a rhythm, which makes a tune more interesting.

Beats work well when all the numbers add up to a whole number — 1, 2, and so on. They don't have to, but strange things happen if you try to play tunes with a different number of beats at the same time.

Live coding

Sonic Pi is designed for *live coding* — which means you can try out sounds and note patterns without stopping other sounds and note patterns.

Take a Guided Tour

After you've made some noise, take a look at the features you can see in the Sonic Pi window.

Look at the code window

The code window is where you write music. The code window is an editor for Sonic Pi code.

Simple? It is. But notice the Workspace buttons under the window. You can edit up to eight projects at the same time. Click a workspace button to swap between projects.

Does that mean you can play eight projects at the same time? Yes, it does! That's why live coding is so cool — you can make an entire band out of software and make each part start, stop, or play something different.

If you make a mistake in your code, Sonic Pi makes a special window appear under the code window, with some cryptic messages to tell you more about why your code doesn't work. The messages aren't easy to understand, but sometimes they give you enough of a clue to fix the problem. You can see an example in Figure 7-4.

Look at the log window

The log window shows messages from Sonic Pi. When Sonic Pi plays a note, it adds a message to the window. When you know more about Sonic Pi, you can write your own messages to the window as reminders to yourself.

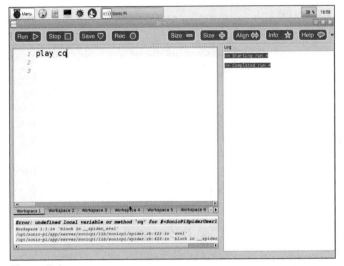

Figure 7-4

Mostly you can ignore what happens in this window. It's not essential reading.

Understand the Help windows

At the bottom of the screen is a Help window. It has two sections.

The small window at the left is a list of all the features in Sonic Pi, collected into groups.

When you click a feature in the left window, the bigger window at the right shows more information about it.

Here's a list of groups:

- **Tutorial:** Step-by-step lessons you can try.

- **Examples:** Ready-made projects.

- **Synths:** Ready-made electronic sounds to make bass notes, bells, whooshes, beeps, growls, and other noises.

- **FX:** Ready-made electronic sound changers that process the sound and make it more interesting. (Or turn it into a grungey distorted mess. But sometimes you want that, so it's cool.)

✔ **Samples:** A different collection of ready-made sounds. Unlike synths, which make sounds by doing lots of scary math, *samples* are recordings of drum sounds, looped rhythms, ambient sounds for atmosphere, and the like.

✔ **Lang:** Short for Language — this section lists all the commands and special words you can use in Sonic Pi code.

On a small screen, you can see only some of the groups. If you move the mouse to the top of the Help bar, the cursor changes into a double arrow. Now you can drag the top of the Help window up and down to show more of the help topics and less of the code window.

Figure 7-5 shows a much bigger Help window.

You can listen to the Tutorial and Example code. Click-drag the mouse to highlight the code — it's red in the tutorials, blue in the examples. Right-click and choose Copy. Select a blank workspace, right-click, and choose paste. Then click Run. To clear a workspace, right-click, choose Clear All, and press Delete.

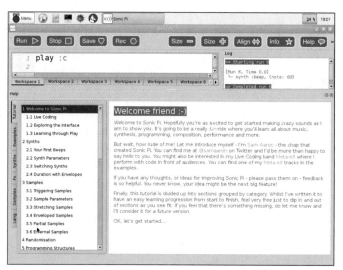

Figure 7-5

Understand the Tools

The Tools along the top of the window control the main features of Sonic Pi. Most tools do more or less what you expect. A few have some not-so-obvious gotcha features:

- **Run:** Play the code in the current workspace.

- **Stop:** Stop all sound in all workspaces.

- **Save:** Save the code in the current workspace. Unfortunately, there's no Load option yet, although it's planned for a future version. So ignore this button for now.

- **Rec:** Record the sound. When you click Stop, Sonic Pi asks for a filename so that you can save the file.

- **Size + and Size -:** Make the code in the window bigger or smaller. This doesn't change the sound; it just makes it easier/harder to see/edit the code.

- **Align:** Apply some magic to make code in the workspace line up the way it should.

- **Info:** Shows an info window about Sonic Pi. You won't need to click this more than once.

- **Help:** Shows/hides the Help area.

- **Prefs:** Set up sound on the Pi. If you use the Pi with a small screen, you can see this button only if you click the double arrows at the far right of the Tools area.

If you're not careful, you can make the Tools disappear. To make them reappear, click on the bar to the right of Log in the Log window and choose Tools in the menu that appears.

As of version 2.4 of Sonic Pi, you can't save and load code. This is a big problem! Supposedly, this feature will appear in version 3. In the meantime, there is a workaround. You can copy and paste code to and from the Leaf editor to save it and reload it. It's not a convenient fix, but it does the job.

Understanding code completion

When you type a command into the code window, Sonic Pi tries to guess the rest of it. It doesn't make very smart guesses — it shows possible code alphabetically in a floating menu next to the code.

You can either scroll through the menu with the mouse to pick a command, or you can keep typing to narrow down the options. When the menu highlights the command you want, press Enter, and Sonic Pi types the rest of it for you. Figure 7-6 shows the floating menu.

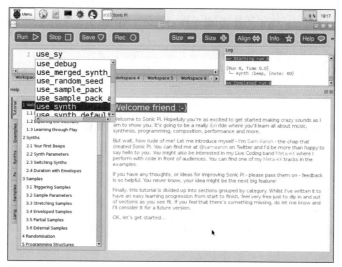

Figure 7-6

This feature is called *code completion.* Many of the code editors used by professional developers include it. It can be a real time-saver, so it's a good idea to get used to working with it.

Understand Music and Sound

You don't need to know a lot about music to make sounds with Sonic Pi, but it helps to know what the different features do.

Use note numbers

Music is made of notes. You can tell Sonic Pi which notes to play in more than one way.

Note numbers have a range of 0 to 127. You don't usually use note numbers lower than 24 because they sound muddy — or so low you can't hear them! Note numbers over 100 are so high they can hurt your ears.

Tunes often sound good with numbers between 40 and 70. This is just a rough guide, not a rule.

Note numbers don't have to be whole numbers. You can do this:

```
play 59.95
play 60
play 60.05
```

Playing groups of note numbers with small differences is a good way to make big, thick, interesting sounds.

If you use bigger differences, the notes sound out of tune.

Music with bigger offsets is called *microtonal*. It's used by expert composers who want to create a very unusual sound and mood.

Use note names

If you know something about music, you can use the usual note letter names ABCDEFG by putting a colon in front of them, like this:

```
play :e
```

You can add a number between 0 and 10, called an *octave*, which makes the pitch lower or higher.

```
play :e2
play :e5
```

Octaves have a weird magic property. In a mysterious way, notes with the same letter are the same note, even though they have a different pitch.

You can also add a *sharp* (s) to make the pitch a little higher or a *flat* (b) to make the pitch a little lower:

```
play :c
play :cs
play :cb
```

Use synths

To make music in Sonic Pi, you use code to pick and play notes and then you send the notes to synths or samples to make a sound.

To use a synth, the command is

```
use_synth :synth_name
```

Click the Synths tab in the left help window to see a list of names. Each synth has a different sound. Experiment with them to hear what they sound like

The colon goes before the synth name, with no space. It doesn't go on the end of use_synth. You'll probably get this wrong a few times before you remember it.

You can make little tunes by playing the same note with different synths:

```
use_synth :fm
play 60
sleep 0.25
use_synth :mod_beep
play 60
sleep 0.25
use_synth :growl
```

```
play 60
sleep 0.25
use_synth :hollow
play 60
```

Using synth parameters

Synth sounds aren't fixed. Synths have settings, called *parameters,* that change the sound. Some settings are standard, and they work on all — or most — synths. Some are unique to each synth.

To play with parameters, add them to a note, like this:

```
play 60, amp: 0.1
```

The amp parameter makes the sound louder or quieter.

If you want to use more parameters, separate them with commas:

```
play 60, amp: 0.1, pan: -1
```

Table 7-2 has a list of parameters that work on most synths. Attack, Decay, and Release take a time in seconds, from 0 to however long you want to wait.

Table 7-2	Sort-of Standard Synth Parameters
Parameter Name	**What Does It Do? What's the Range?**
Amp	Sets the volume: 0 to 1
Pan	Moves the sound between the speakers: –1 to 1
Attack	Controls how quickly the sound starts
Decay	Controls how quickly the sound reaches the sustain volume after it starts
Sustain	Volume after the decay time: 0 to 1
Release	Controls how quickly the sound dies away

TIP

You can make sounds that take minutes to get started and hours to die away. They're not very fun to listen to, but if you want to do it, Sonic Pi makes it possible.

Understand default parameters

Synths have parameter settings baked in. When you play a synth, it uses these default numbers for its settings, unless you add your own settings to a note.

To see a list of parameters and default settings, click the Synth tab in the left help window and click any synth from the list. The boxes under the name show all the parameter names you can use for that synth and the default settings for each parameter.

For example, if you look up the synth called dsaw, Figure 7-7 shows that the default sustain value is 0, the default cutoff is 100, and so on.

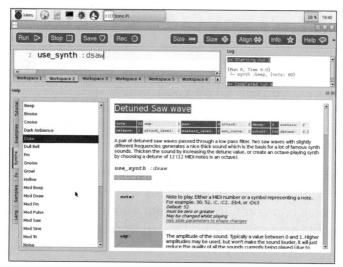

Figure 7-7

If you don't know what a parameter does, try playing it with different settings to see how the sound changes. Synth parameter names are based on those used in hardware synthesizers and in electronic music plug-ins. If you want to know more, you can try searching for the parameter name online.

Make More Complicated Music

You know enough now to start making simple tracks. You can create some very cool effects just by switching synths and changing parameters, even if you play the same note over and over.

If you know more about music, you can pick note numbers and letter names to make tunes and play lots of notes together to make chords.

Sonic Pi includes some features to save typing. Instead of copying and pasting a section, you can write some simple code to repeat it. You can also use a range of other sounds to make more interesting music.

Take some time to experiment with synths, notes, and settings and see what you can do on your own.

There are no mistakes; there's only more or less interesting music to make.

 If you want to know more about music, you can find a massive amount of information online about *music theory,* which tells you how to pick and combine notes and make rhythms. It's a huge subject, but you can pick up the bare essentials in an evening or two.

Week 3
Finding Out More about Programming

In this part, you'll . . .

Don't forget to check out the online articles and bonus chapters at www.dummies.com/extras/raspberrypiforkids.

Get Started with Python

Computer experts enjoy creating new programming languages. While you literally have hundreds of languages to choose from, at any given time, only a few are popular.

This project introduces a popular language called Python. Unlike some programming languages, Python is easy to learn and use. But it's also a real grown-up language used by grown-ups for real work. If you learn Python, you'll be on your way to creating software you can sell.

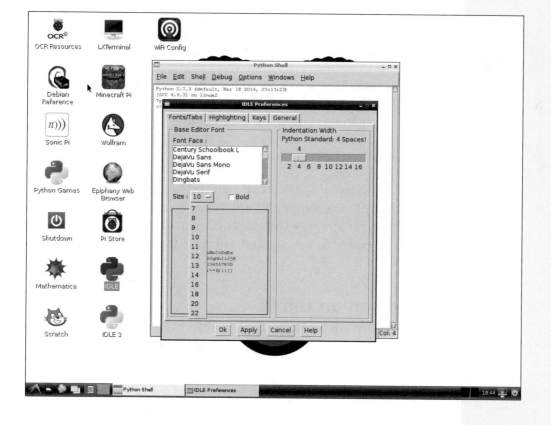

Meet Python

Scratch is a good way to start learning about making computers do what you want, but it's just a beginning. There's a lot you can't do with Scratch. For example, you can't create your own desktop windows, search web pages for information, or send Tweets.

For bigger and smarter projects, you need a bigger and smarter way to give your computer instructions, which you can do in lots of ways. One of the most popular methods is to type your instructions using a *programming language*. A programming language takes your instructions and tries to understand them. If your instructions make sense, the programming language tells the chips and other parts of the computer what they need to do.

Programming languages save you time because you don't have to think about all the complicated things the computer is doing while it works. You can use instructions that look a bit like English, and the programming language does the rest.

Although Scratch is a very simple programming language, it's very unusual. Most languages don't give you instruction blocks you can clip together. Instead, you write *commands* — special words that tell the computer what you want it to do. The list of commands you write is called *code*.

To make a program, you type code on the keyboard into an *editor*. An editor is a bit like a notepad application or a word processor, but it has special features to help you write code. Some editors can even run code for you so that you can check whether it works right away.

Find Python on the Pi

A version of Python with a matching editor is included in Raspbian. It appears on the desktop as IDLE, as shown in Figure 8-1.

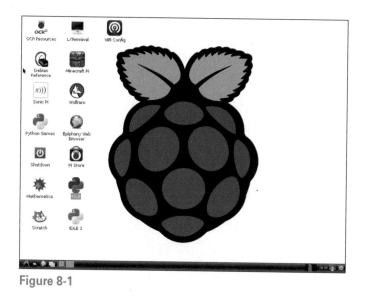

Figure 8-1

The figures in this project use the older Pi desktop, so you can see what it looks like in case you buy a memory card with an older version of NOOBS. You can find the newer Pi desktop throughout the rest of this book. Python works the same way on both desktops.

To get started with Python, do the following:

1. **Power up your Pi, if isn't already running.**

2. **If you don't have the desktop open, type `startx` and press Enter to launch it.**

3. **Find the icon labeled IDLE.**

If you look very, very carefully, you'll find an icon labeled IDLE 3. Ignore it. It launches a different kind of Python. If you try to use it, some of the code in this book won't work. This will make both of us unhappy, so don't click that icon!

4. **Double-click the icon.**

You should see a window labeled Python Shell, as shown in Figure 8-2.

On the newer desktop, click the Menu button at the top right and choose Programming⇨Python 2. Ignore Python 3!

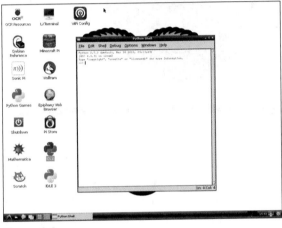

Figure 8-2

In computer-land, shells have nothing to do with the sea. You use a shell to tell the computer what to do. Here, you use the Python shell to tell Python what to do. The shell includes an editor for code, but you can also use it to send simple commands to Python. The shell runs them and shows you what Python does with them.

You've likely noticed that the date at the top of the window isn't the current date. It's the date when the people who made Python released it into the world for everyone to use. Some people get confused by this date, so it's good to unconfuse them.

Set up Python

Before you try using Python, you can make the text in the editor bigger and easier to read. You can skip this step if you have a wall-sized monitor and can see the text just fine. Otherwise, do the following:

1. **In the menu at the top of the Python Shell window, click Options.**

2. **Click Configure IDLE, as shown in Figure 8-3.**

   The Idle Preferences window appears.

Figure 8-3

3. **In the Font tab, click the Size box.**

4. **Click a number in the drop-down list, as shown in Figure 8-4.**

   The *default* size — the one that's preselected for you — is 10. To make the text bigger, select a bigger number. The Python examples in this book use 14 to make them easy to read on the page. That size may be too big for you. Try setting the size to 12 first.

5. **Click Ok to set the new size.**

   When you change the text size, the text gets bigger, and the window gets bigger, too.

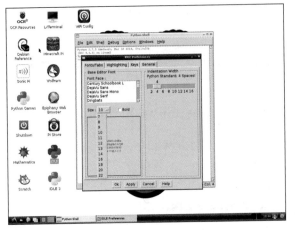

Figure 8-4

If you set a really big text size you'll get a window that may not fit on the screen. This doesn't usually cause issues, but it can look kind of weird and disturbing. If the window is toooooo wiiiiide, you can't see all the text in it, which is not what you want.

Unleash Python math power

Now you can unleash the full power of Python supercomputing. The line with the angle brackets is called a *prompt*. It's like the Linux command prompt, except that it sends commands to Python instead of Linux.

Type the following at the prompt and then press Enter:

```
>>>1+1
```

Woo hoo! Python instantly solves this tough problem, as you can see in Figure 8-5.

Obviously, Python can do harder math. Try something like

>>>1/81.0*100

Don't forget to press Enter. You'll see that Python has no problem with more complicated sums.

Figure 8-5

Python is more accurate than a basic calculator. Try the same sum on a calculator, and you get a shorter and less precise answer. This small difference doesn't matter for simple classroom math, but some college-level math problems need very accurate answers. A calculator isn't good enough — but Python is.

Make mistakes

Figure 8-6 shows what happens when the shell can't understand what you want — either because you made a mistake or because you tried to confuse it, like I did here. Although it's totally not obvious, the weird message that appears means "I didn't understand that last command. Try again."

Python can show all kinds of error messages. When you've used Python for a while, you can see the messages are trying to give you useful hints. Until then, they're hard to understand because they look kind of random. This problem occurs in most programming languages. When something goes wrong and you see error messages, they look like weird not-quite-English. They're often not as clear and helpful as maybe they could be.

Figure 8-6

Remember Information

Programming languages spend a lot of time remembering information. In most languages, including Python, you remember things by making imaginary boxes to store the information. You have to give each box a different name so that you don't get them mixed up.

Boxes hold one piece of information at a time. You can change what's in a box, and you can open the lid to see what's inside it.

As a simple start, store a number in a box. (You can also store words in boxes, but words need special code, so don't try that yet.)

In computer-speak, boxes are called *variables*. This is a big, scary word, but it just means a box with something in it.

When you learn more about Python, you'll see that you can put boxes inside other boxes to make collections. Often, it's useful to do something to lots of boxes at the same time. It's much easier to do this if you put them in a collection. Otherwise, you end up with boxes all over the floor and a giant mess.

Make a variable

To make a variable and put a number inside it, type the following and then press Enter:

```
my_number = 1
```

You can maybe guess what this does: It makes a box called `my_number` and puts 1 in it.

The line between the two words in the box name is called an *underscore.* It's not the same as minus sign. If you type a minus sign by mistake, Python gets confused. On most keyboards, you can type an underscore by holding down the Shift key and pressing the key with the minus sign.

If you don't make any mistakes, Python swallows this code, and nothing much seems to happen. Python shows a prompt on a new line and carries on waiting.

But if you type

```
print my_number
```

and press Enter again, Python looks through its box collection to find the box called `my_number`. Then it shows the value you told it to remember, as shown in Figure 8-7.

Variables are variable, so if you type

```
my_number = 2
```

press Enter and then check what's in `my_number` now, you'll see you've successfully put 2 in it, as shown in Figure 8-7.

The `print` command doesn't print on paper — it prints on the screen. In the shell, you don't have to type `print` to look inside a box. It's included here to make the examples clearer. But if you're in a hurry, you can leave it out and just type the variable name. This works only in the shell! In the editor, you have to use `print` when you want Python to show you what's inside a variable.

Figure 8-7

Use variables

Why waste time putting numbers in boxes? Here's a neat magic trick: You can tell Python to do math on numbers in boxes. Type the following (and don't forget to press Enter at the end of every line):

```
my_other_number = 10
my_number*my_other_number
```

Python does its calculator thing on the numbers in the boxes.

This is HUGE! It means that when you have lots of variables and all kinds of information, you can combine everything in complicated ways.

For example, instead of adding up a list of numbers by hand, you can give them to Python, and it can do the sum for you. If any of the numbers change, you can change the value in one box and tell Python to redo the sum.

You don't have to type all the numbers again. Awesome!

Make recipes

You have gained your first computer superpowers. You can make boxes, put values in them, and do math on them. One final god-like trick is to put the value of math you do into a new box, like this:

```
my_big_number = my_number * my_other_number
```

In computer-speak, use the * symbol when you want to multiply numbers. It's usually above the number 9 on the number pad on your keyboard, or on Shift + 8. Don't use *x* or *X* because Python will think you're trying to do something with text or letters or something, and it won't work.

This one line of code is beyond awesome. You've made a *recipe* for working with information. You don't need to know what's in the boxes. The code just works as long as the variables hold numbers. It doesn't care what the numbers are. It works for *all* of them.

The catch is that you can't multiply words, collections, photos, or music!

Writing a computer program often means making a list of recipes. For example, instead of doing math on specific numbers, you can make a list of math recipes. Then you can use them over and over whenever you need some math to happen.

This is why computers are so useful. You can build recipes that do useful things to almost any kind of information — not just numbers, but words, videos, music tracks, web pages, and pictures of cats being cute and dogs falling off skateboards.

In computer-speak, recipes are called *algorithms* — maybe because calling them recipes doesn't sound serious and grown-up enough. It's always better to use a difficult word when you want to look grown-up.

Use the Shell and the Editor

Wasn't IDLE supposed to be a code editor? How do you type and edit code in the shell? What does the shell do anyway?

In the shell window, you type code line by line directly into Python. When you press Enter, the shell checks whether your code makes sense. If it does, it sends it to Python. If Python returns a result — like the answer to a basic math problem — it shows it in the window.

In outline, the shell recipe looks like this:

1. **Show the prompt and wait for the user to type a command and press Enter.**

2. **Read in the command.**

3. **Check if it makes sense.**

4. **If there's a problem, complain to the user and go to Step 7; if everything is fine, send the command to Python and continue to Step 5.**

5. **Wait for Python to run the command and return a result.**

6. **If there's a result, show it in the shell window.**

7. **Show the prompt and wait again.**

You don't need to remember this list. The point here is that the shell is a computer program. The creators of Python had to sketch out a list like this so they knew what the shell had to do. Then they wrote code for each step to make it work.

Python is really, really complicated on the inside. But when you make your own programs, it's a good idea to sketch out the steps for your code before you start.

A sketch of steps is sometimes called a *specification.* It's like a recipe for the entire program, but it doesn't include the code that makes each step work. A good specification outlines everything a program does. It even includes all the things that can go wrong, so the program is smart enough to handle mistakes made by human users.

A specification is a bit like a map you can use to find your way around the code. Each block of code does a small and simple thing. When you put all the blocks together, they do something big, complicated, and clever — like running Python, making a big website work, managing all the apps in your phone, or making sure your microwave makes popcorn without bursting into flames and burning down the house.

Open the Editor window

What if you want to run a series of commands without having to type them one by one? You can also do this in IDLE, but you have to open the editor window first.

To open it, choose File ⇨ New Window. Figure 8-8 shows the result. When you open a new editor window, it's labeled Untitled. It's completely blank, with no prompt, and the menu options are different.

Figure 8-8

Add code

To write code, type it into the window. As usual, press Enter at the end of each line. The editor doesn't try to run your code. It just moves the text cursor to the next line.

To keep things simple, type code based on the commands in the rest of this project. Make a couple of variables, put numbers in them, and do some simple math on them. Include a print command to show the result.

Figure 8-9 shows some possible code, which I also list here so that you don't have to squint at the page:

```
my_number = 1234
my_other_number = 5678
my_product = my_number * my_other_number
print my_product
```

Figure 8-9

 When you type, the editor highlights words that Python recognizes in red. Python doesn't recognize your variables names because you invented them. It does recognize print because it's a Python command.

Run code

How do you send the code to Python to run it? Click Run ⇨ Run Module F5 or press F5 on your keyboard.

And, nope, you still can't run it. That's because you have to save the code first. If you haven't saved it, Python nags you with an alert box. Click OK in the alert box to open a save dialog box, shown in Figure 8-10.

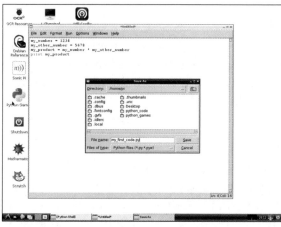

Figure 8-10

The file selector points to your home directory in Linux. If you logged in as the usual Pi user, this is /home/pi.

Type a file name and click the Save button. Python files need a .py extension. Remember to include it. For example, you might name the file my_first_code.py.

If you're lazy you could name it a.py, but then you'll come back to your home directory a few months from now and wonder what all the Python projects you named a.py, b.py, c.py … do.

Unfortunately, you can't create directories in the file selector. This is a bad thing, but it's how it is. If you want to keep all your Python projects in a directory — a good idea, but not totally essential — click Cancel in the file selector and open the desktop

File Manager. Create a new directory called `python_code` in `/home/pi`. Include the underscore and don't use a space because it makes it easier to use the directory from the Linux command line.

Click the Save button. Python switches to the shell window and displays a big RESTART message. If your code doesn't have any mistakes, you'll see a number like the one Python works out and displays the answer. The number you get depends on the numbers in your code and the math you did with them.

Check code

If you made a mistake, click the editor window and look at your code again. Did you leave out an underscore or use a minus sign instead? Did you mistype the variable names so that they don't match where they should? Did you use an X instead a *? Did you add any extra letters or characters? Did you put all your code on one line?

Computers are super-picky. Python doesn't care how you spell variable names. yo_sup_dawg, bannnnnnnnnana and ftryurgh will all work. But if you don't use *exactly* the same names throughout your code, with exactly the same spelling and underscores, Python gets very confused.

Near enough isn't good enough. Exactly means exactly the same. No exceptions. (Did I mention that already?)

Make a Guessing Game with Python

Chapter 8 introduces the Python programming language. This chapter explains how to make a simple number guessing game for one player. The player thinks of a number between 1 and 10. Your code guesses the number.

Sounds simple, right?

Not so fast. You have to think about *everything* that can happen in the game. And you also have to discover more about Python.

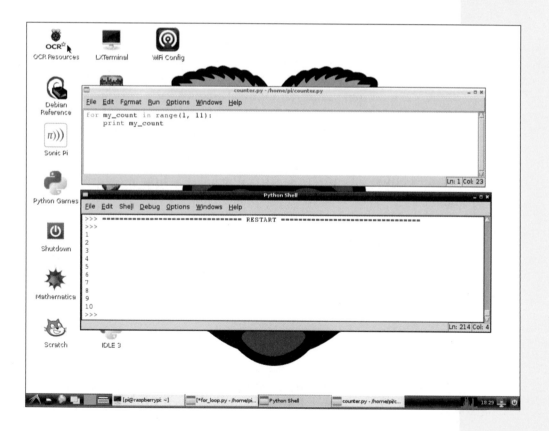

Think about Code

Does having to think about code mean you're a terrible programmer?

No!

It's *good*. It means you have to think about what you're doing. Good programmers do a *lot* of thinking before they start writing and typing code. They start by breaking a big and complicated problem into small steps. Then they work through the steps.

Good programmers have to learn new tricks all the time. You might think developers already know everything they need to know.

It would be cool if they did. But that's not what happens.

Software developers have to learn new things all the time. Sometimes this means looking up how to do things in a new language — like Python. Sometimes it means finding out whether someone else has invented a clever answer for a problem. And sometimes it means looking at the code and projects that other developers are working on to see whether you can learn anything from them.

So not knowing where to start is normal. It's how most projects begin.

Work out what you need to learn

For a project like the one in this chapter, you have to sketch out how your game works in outline, without worrying about clever details.

This part is easy. Most computer software has the same shape. It looks like this:

1. **Ask the user a question, wait for the user to click or tap a button, or load some information from a file.**

2. **Check that the user hasn't made a mistake.**

3. **Do something useful or clever.**

   For this game, it means working out how to guess a number.

4. **Show a response and/or save it to a new file.**

5. **Check whether you're done yet.**

6. **If you're done, stop; otherwise, go back to Step 1 and go around again.**

Most games wait until the user pushes a button on a hand controller or clicks a control on the screen. When something happens, the game responds by updating the position of the spaceship, or the treasure, or the cute talking candy, and maybe increasing the score — unless the spaceship blows up, a unicorn from the other team steals the treasure, or the candy disappears, in which case sound effects and sad music happen, and the player has to start again.

In computer-land, information from the outside world is called the *input.* The software takes the input, and after doing clever things to it, it produces an *output.* Information in general is called *data,* which means whatever you're given to work with. Doing something clever is called *processing the data.* So the short version of the loop is input⇨processing⇨output.

Make a list of things to do

After you have an outline (see Figure 9-1), you can work out what you need to learn. Make a list of your own first, and see how much it looks like the one here:

🠶 How do I ask my player a question in Python?

🠶 How do I get an answer from my player?

🠶 How do I check that the answer makes sense?

 ✔ How do I guess a number in a clever way?

 ✔ How do I know when we're done?

 ✔ How do I make my code loop back?

 ✔ How do I stop?

How Software Works

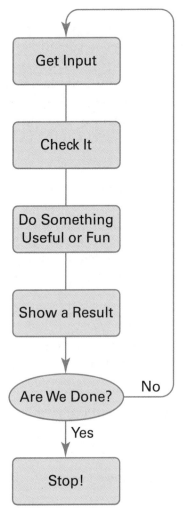

Figure 9-1

That's a lot of questions for a simple game!

But wait! You don't have to answer them all at once! You can take them one at a time. Suddenly that doesn't look like such a huge job. It's still a big job, but it's not impossibly planet-sized in a too-big kind of a way.

Breaking down one hard problem like "Make a cool game" into lots of simple problems like "How do I stop?" is the only way to go. Trying to get all the parts of a game working as you type is like jumping into an alligator pit and trying to fight all the alligators at once with one hand tied to a mouse and the other tied to your head.

Taking things step by step means you can write code for each question without worrying about the other questions.

Doing everything at once will only confuse you, and give the alligators an unfair advantage. You don't want that — even if you like alligators.

 Some books about software list the code you should type, and then — if you're lucky — they explain a little about how it works. Doing it this way looks easy, but it doesn't teach you how to write your own code. Asking questions and thinking first looks much harder, but once you get over the scary part at the beginning, you'll write better code more quickly, and you'll be less likely to get stuck.

Ask the Player a Question

How do you ask the player a question in Python? How do you find out how to ask a question?

Search on the web! Open the Epiphany web browser on your Pi — see Chapter 5 for details and type Python ask question into the search bar at the top. Figure 9-2 shows the results you may see. (You may not get exactly the same results, but you should see similar hits.)

Figure 9-2

Why not search for Ask a question in Python? Sometimes full English questions work just fine, but sometimes they confuse the search engine, so it's better not to use them while searching.

Search engines are kind of dumb, and they don't understand English questions. They just look for important words, so you can leave out words that don't matter, like *a* and *the* and *of*. And you get better answers by putting the most important word first. In this example, that's Python. That's how you get "Python ask question."

When you search for answers to Python questions, you'll see a lot of links to two sites. Don't visit them yet! `http://docs.python.org` is the official Python manual and guide. `http://stackoverflow.com` is a site where grown-up developers ask and answer questions. You can come back to these sites when you've spent more time with Python. They have too much detail when you're starting out — and on stackoverflow, the grown-ups disagree with each other a lot, which may not help you find what you need.

Using raw_input

Take some time to look through the top hits. Do you see how to ask a question and get an answer now? Searching the web tells you the answer: You can use a Python command called `raw_input` to get an answer from a user.

You need to add some code that looks something like this:

```
player_answer = raw_input("Question: yes or no?")
```

 You can also combine `print` and `raw_input` on a single line, separated by a comma. But you don't really need to use `print`. If you include your question between (round brackets) and "quote marks", `raw_input` prints it on the screen anyway.

Test your new skill

It's always good to test code as you go. Sometimes it's easier to write a test as a small side project.

To test your question-asking code:

1. **Choose File ⇨ New Window to open a new Editor window.**

2. **Type the following:**

   ```
   player_answer = raw_input("What is your answer? ")
   print "Your answer was: " + player_answer
   ```

3. **Save the file as `question_answer.py` and run it.**

   If you didn't make any typos, you should see something like the messages in Figure 9-3.

`raw_input` doesn't care what the user types. It's like a dumb robot. If you type a load of gibberish, it saves the gibberish in the `player_answer` variable.

The next line in the code prints out whatever is in `player_answer`. It doesn't care if it's gibberish either.

Figure 9-3

But hey, you've ticked off two whole items on your to-do list! You know how to ask the user a question and how to get an answer.

Working out whether the answer makes sense is a *different problem*.

This is why it's so cool to break any big project into lots of teeny problems. You can make progress by working on them one at a time.

Why is there a + in the second line? Because you can join two bits of text together with a +. The print command glues the two bits together because of the + and makes them appear on one line. (You can't do math on text, and this isn't *really* math. It just looks a bit like math. Sort of.)

Check the Answer

To check whether an answer makes sense, you need to know the difference between a good answer and a bad answer.

In this example, you're making a guessing game, so to keep it simple, you want very simple answers to questions — yes or no. If the player types anything else, your code should ignore it.

But it can't just ignore it and carry on. It has to keep asking the question over and over until the player types yes or no. So the check has to include a test that loops back to ask the question again until it gets an answer that works.

Now you have to replace one old problem (How do I check the answer makes sense?) with two new problems:

✔ How do I check whether an answer is yes or no?

✔ How do I keep asking the question until the answer is yes or no?

Isn't that more work? Yes, it is. But you often have to keep splitting a problem into smaller problems. It's not unusual to find that your project to-do list gets bigger for a while as you work through it.

It gets smaller eventually. Promise!

 If you were making a bigger game, you would have to keep splitting problems into smaller problems over and over. Really big games, like Angry Birds, Candy Crush, or Grand Theft Auto, are made of *thousands* of problems — too many problems for one person to work out. Teams of developers work on them together for years, but they still do what you're doing here: breaking down a big problem into lots of small problems and writing code to solve them, one by one.

Check for yes or no

If you spent some time playing with Scratch, you'll know there are two ways to check whether something is true. You can use if , like this:

```
if something is true
    do a thing
else
    do some other thing
```

Or you can use `repeat...until`, like this:

```
repeat
     do a thing
until
     some test is true
```

`if` solves half the problem. You could use it to check for yes or no, but it doesn't give you a way to keep asking the same question over and over.

`repeat...until` sounds perfect. It checks and loops at the same time, like this:

```
repeat
     answer=raw_input("Question...")
until
     answer = "yes" or answer = "no"
```

The question keeps appearing until the answer is yes or no. Perfect!

But, uh, unfortunately, Python doesn't understand `repeat... until`.

Also — wait a minute. . . .

Doesn't

```
     answer = "yes"
```

mean you're saving a value of yes in the `answer` variable? That's not much use as a check, is it?

If you spotted this is wrong, you are well on your way to being a computer genius! Good job! If you didn't, don't worry. Most people miss it. In fact, some developers forget it, even if they've been writing software for years.

Check for anything at all

You have to know the magic word to check whether two things are the same. The magic word is two equals signs instead of one, like this:

```
repeat
    do really cool stuff
until
    answer == "yes" or answer == "no"
```

Why? This is one of those times where *it just is*. It's a magic word, and you have to know it. That's all.

Go around and around . . .

So that's half the problem solved. What can you use in Python to do the same job as `repeat...until`?

If you do a web search, you'll see it's called `while`. It works like this:

```
while [include a test here]
    do cool stuff
    do more cool stuff
carry on from here...
```

Cool stuff happens over and over while the result of the test is true. The code keeps doing the cool stuff until the test is false/not true. Then Python moves on to whatever happens next.

Problem solved? Nearly. But not quite.

Check for opposites

Here's a question for you: When should the code loop? What tests should you put in `while`?

Look at Table 9-1 to help you guess.

Table 9-1   When Should My Code Loop and Ask Again?

Is the Answer Yes?	Is the Answer No?	Should I Ask Again?
Yes	Doesn't matter	No
Doesn't matter	Yes	No
No	No	Yes!

The code should loop while the player's answer isn't yes, *and* it isn't no.

This point will either seem, like, *totally obvious,* or it will seem brain-meltingly weird. Some people are fine with the idea of checking for two things that aren't true. Others find it harder. If it seems hard, skip to the code and don't think too much about the logic.

How do you check whether something isn't equal to something else? You need another magic word. It looks like this:

```
if answer != "yes"
```

In English, when you see != you say not equal. So the code checks whether the answer is not the same as, not equal to, and generally different to yes — which is exactly what you want.

The `while` test looks like this:

```
answer = raw_input("Question: yes or no? ")
while answer != "yes" and answer != "no":
    answer = raw_input("Question: yes or no? ")
```

You have to set up the test to fail before you go into the loop, to make sure `raw_input` happens at least once. You could make it blank, but it's just as easy to ask for some useful input and check it.

The officially approved way to use a `while` loop in Python looks different. It starts with `while True:` followed by code that does the cool stuff you want done. The version here works just as well and is simpler. Often there's more than one way to write code that works. The right way depends on tradition, style, and how big and scary your boss and/or teacher is.

Add colons and indentation

You also have to put a colon (":") after the test. Python needs to see a colon after every test in your code. (It's another of those "Because reasons" magic word features.)

When you end a line with a colon, the Editor automatically, at no extra cost to you, *indents* the next line, adding a gap of a few spaces at the start.

Python uses the extra spaces to remember that the indented code goes under the `while`. If it didn't do this, it wouldn't know which code to skip after the `while`, and it would get very confused about what it was supposed to do.

Figure 9-4 shows a slightly remixed and expanded version of the same code. The variable is called `player_answer` for clarity, but it works just like the code on the previous page.

As you can see, you can type any old nonsense and the code keeps asking you for yes or no, relentlessly, like a Terminator robot. It gives up only when you enter yes or no.

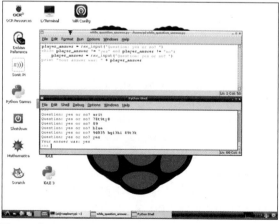

Figure 9-4

Woo hoo! It works! But that was a lot of work for a simple thing, wasn't it?

It's normal for software to spend a lot of time checking the input. Humans are unpredictable, but good software can handle every possible thing a human might do. This can take a long time to get right because there are soooooo many possibilities.

Humans are also sneaky. Important websites, especially shopping and banking sites, have to be even more careful about checking to make sure that hackers can't get in. Otherwise, the hackers will steal all the credit card numbers they can find and buy truckloads of nice things for themselves and their friends. (This is not a joke. It really happens.)

Repeat Questions

The code is almost ready to start making a simple version of the game. You could make it ask questions like this:

```
Think of a number between 1 and 10!
Is your number 1 (yes or no)?
Is your number 2 (yes or no)?
Is your number 3 (yes or no)?
```

And so on for all the other numbers, up to

```
Is your number 10 (yes or no)?
```

This version of the game always guesses the right number. It's not very interesting, magical, or fun. But it works.

It's fine to make code do simple not-quite-finished things, especially while you're learning new stuff. So think of this early version as a super-secret experiment. You don't have to show it to anyone. Getting it working is still an achievement to be proud of, and you can add extra cleverness and magic later.

Count to ten

How do you count to ten? There's more than one way to make your code do this. You could put another `while` loop around the code, starting with a guess of 1, adding 1 to the guess each time, and breaking out of the loop when the guess is 11.

But if you've played with Scratch, you know a different way, called a `for` loop. Unlike a `while` loop, a `for` loop includes a variable that holds a count. The counter works automatically. Every time your code goes around the `for` loop, the value in the counter gets bigger by one.

Use range in Python

`for` loops in Python are slightly weird. Instead of saying "Start from this number and end with that number" you have to give Python a range.

Here's an example that counts from one to ten:

```
for my_count in range(1, 11):
    print my_count
```

This is almost easy to understand. In English, it would say, "Count from the start of the range (1) to the end of the range (11) and print the count each time through."

But why is the last number of the range 11 and not 10? Because reasons! This is another of those things in Python that doesn't really make sense. You just have to remember that when you use a `for` loop, the end of the `range` is always one more than you'd expect.

Figure 9-5 shows that you can now count to ten in Python.

All computer programming languages do some stuff that makes no sense. Python is better than most. But all languages have at least a few things that make you think "Huh? What? Why?" when you see them. When this happens, you just have to deal.

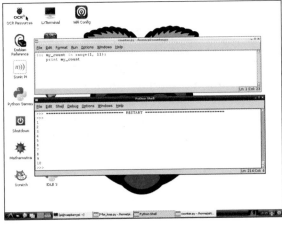

Figure 9-5

Stop the count early

What if you want to stop the count early? What if your game guesses the number before reaching ten?

You can jump out of a `for` loop with a magic word called `break`, like this:

```
for my_count in range(1, 11):
    print my_count
    if my_count == 4:
        break
```

When `my_count` is 4, the `for` loop screeches to a halt with the sound of squealing brakes and the smell of burning rubber.

Not literally. It would be fun if it did. But no.

However, it does stop early. Sometimes that's what you want.

Figure Out Variable Types

Remember, you can't do math on text. And you can't join numbers together to make words and sentences.

This means not all variables are the same. And this won't work:

```
for my_count in range(1, 11):
    print "This number is: " + my_count
```

When Python prints a single variable, it makes a best guess about what you want to see. You can use `print` with a number, or with text, and it works fine.

But Python is kind of dumb. It isn't smart enough to glue text to a number and make it work. So when you try to `print` text *and a* number on the same line, Python has a meltdown and sulks.

Just to confuse you, you can remember numbers in Python in two different ways. You can remember them as whole numbers, which is a good way to count things or say "The fifth item in a list."

Or you can go the whole shebang and remember them with a decimal point, which is the right option when you need to do serious math.

Python also remembers text. Text is just letters, spaces, and all those weird characters on your computer keyboard.

You can remember numbers as text — "5.1234" — but to Python, text is always text and is no different than "Awesome!" or "e78tgn-jhtjgkyl6ui". You can't do math on text — not even if it's full of numbers. *It's always just text.*

These three ways to remember data are so useful they have their own names. Tables 9-2 and 9-3 list them for you.

`int` is short for integer, which is math-speak for whole number. `float` is short for floating point number, which is math-speak for a number with a decimal point. `string` is short for text string, which isn't math-speak for anything and has nothing to do with any other kind of string, and especially not the kind you tie things up with.

Table 9-2	A Few Variable Types	
Type Name	**Example**	**Used For**
int	10	Whole numbers only
float	3.14159	Numbers with a decimal point
string	"text"	Letters, words, and sentences

Here's something you need to remember: All the types do math differently. You can't do math on strings, but you can use + to glue one string to another to make a longer string.

float math just works. int math is weird. You can add, subtract, and multiply just fine. But if you divide one int by another, you only get the whole number part of the answer. Any fractions or decimals disappear!

Table 9-3	Math You Can Do	
Type Name	**Math You Can Do**	**Example**
int	Whole number math only (division rounds down)	5 / 2 = 2
float	All math	5 / 2 = 2.5
string	"+" only	"a" + "b" = "ab"

This happens for several reasons. The reasons make sense if you know how computers work under the hood. It takes a lot less time, electricity, and computer memory to do int math than float math. In a really big piece of software, using int where possible saves time and money. So that's why there's a difference. And yes, there are more types — many more. But three is enough to get started.

Convert types

It would be really useful if you could convert between the types. And you can! Python includes a toolkit that does exactly this. Table 9-4 shows you.

Table 9-4	Converting Types	
Conversion Code	What It Does	Example
int(variable)	Makes an int	int(5.9) = 5
float(variable)	Makes a float	float(5) = 5.0
str(variable)	Makes a string	str(1) = "1"

Did you see how `int(5.9)` keeps only the whole number part and throws away the rest? It doesn't try to round up the result to 6. It just trashes everything that isn't a whole number. Beware!

Print text and numbers

You can make the example in the "Repeat Questions" section work. Add `str()` around the counter variable, and suddenly you can combine a number with text:

```
for my_count in range(1, 11):
    print "The count is: " + str(my_count)
```

Put the Guessing Game All Together

Now you can sketch out the simple version of the guessing game, like this:

1. **Use a `for` loop to count from 1 to 10.**

2. **Show the current guess.**

3. **Ask the player to type yes if it's right or no if it's not.**

   Keep asking until the player types yes or no.

4. **If the player said yes, print "I guessed the number!"; otherwise, go back to Step 2 and allow the loop to try the next number.**

What happens if you get to 10, and the player hasn't said yes? Obviously, this scenario is impossible, and the player is a bad person who lies to computers. So you can add one last step:

5. **If the guess gets to 10 and the player hasn't said yes yet, call the player a liar.**

You should know enough about Python now to write the code to make this happen. To save time, here's one possible answer.

```
for guess in range (1,11):
    answer = raw_input("Is your number " +
    str(guess) + " - yes or no? ")
    while answer != "yes" and answer != "no":
        answer = raw_input("Is your number " +
    str(guess) + " - yes or no? ")
    if answer == "yes":
        print "I guessed the number!"
        break
if answer == "no":
    print "You're lying!"
```

Figure 9-6 shows how it works on the Pi.

Figure 9-6

This page isn't wide enough to show the code formatted the way it should be. Look at Figure 9-6 to see how all the spaces and indentations work. If you're too lazy to type the code, you can download it from the book's website.

Repeat Code and Make It Simpler

The code works, but it's kind of complicated and hard to read.

Good code is easy to read, but this code has a lot of detail on some of the lines. And some of the code is repeated.

Repeats are bad because they mean the code isn't as neat as it could be. They also make it harder to change the code. If you change one repeat, you have to change them all. But it's easy to forget a repeat or to make a mistake.

So this code is more likely to have *bugs* — mistakes — than simpler code. And as you keep adding to it, you're more likely to add more bugs.

Python has a neat way to deal with repeats. You can wrap your code inside a *function*.

Does function have anything to do with "private functions" for adults, like weddings? No! It comes from college math, where a *function* is a blob of math that takes an input, does something to it, and makes an output. A lot of names in computer-land escaped from math-land. College math-land is a strange and mysterious place — much stranger than most people think. This is why the words sound so weird and so different to normal English.

Find out about functions

Functions can have four ingredients, although they don't always need them all:

- ✔ A name

- ✔ Input variables

✔ Code to repeat

✔ A way to return a result

You don't always need the input — for example, if you write a function to tell the time, it doesn't need to be told the time. (Duh.)

You don't always need to return a result. But you do always need a unique name, and some code that does something.

The input variable is sometimes called a *parameter,* which is another weird name that fell out of math-land. Functions can have more than one parameter.

Make and use functions

To make a function, you use the magic word def, like this:

```
def my_function(input variables):
    [clever code for the function goes here]
    return output
```

To use the function, type this:

```
some_value = my_function(input)
```

This runs all the clever code, but the function code stays in one place. You also can use it over and over by typing a single line whenever you need it in the rest of the code.

Decide what to put in a function

When you split some code into a function, you want to make the rest of the code easier to read, and you also want to create a block of code you can reuse. Either option is good, but if you can get both, that's a total win.

In this game, it's hard to read the lines with raw_input. You can fix this in two ways.

You can put each `raw_input` line into a function and use the function to replace it.

Or you can take the entire `answer` block of code and put that into a function, like this:

```
for my_guess in range (1,11):
    answer = answer_for_guess(my_guess)
    if answer == "yes":
        print "I guessed the number!"
        break
if answer == "no":
    print "You're lying!"
```

That's a lot easier to read, isn't it? If you remember about breaking down a big problem into smaller problems, you can use functions to help you.

This also means you can sketch out code as a list of functions and then write the code inside them later!

Write a guess function

You're almost ready to write your first function. You need to know that the `def` section goes at the start of the code.

And there's one more thing you can do to make the code simpler. You can put the question string into a variable so that you can repeat it without having to retype it. You don't need to write a function to do this because the string doesn't do any processing.

Figure 9-7 shows how it works:

```
def answer_for_guess(this_guess):
    question_string = "Is your number " + str(this_
    guess) + " - yes or no? "
    answer = raw_input(question_string)
    while answer != yes and answer != no:
        answer = raw_input(question_string)
    return answer
```

Figure 9-7

Variable names get special privileges inside a function. The rule is that whatever happens inside the function stays inside the function, unless you use `return` to return it.

Add Smarts and Magic

There's a secret rule of software design that no one will tell you: Good software seems smarter than you are; bad software seems dumber than you are.

Software is like stage magic. If you can see how the tricks are done, it's kind of disappointing. But if you can't, it's a lot more impressive. And if it's really good, it almost looks like real magic.

So far, this game is not smart. How can you make it smarter? You need a better way to guess numbers. Anyone can count through them one by one.

Can you think of a better way? You could try numbers at random instead of counting — like throwing a ten-sided dice for each guess. But that will take just as long, *and* you'll have to do a lot more work to put your guesses in a random order.

Developers spend a lot of time working out clever and fast ways to do things like sorting and searching through numbers and words. If you're very good at computers, you can guess some of the simpler recipes *(algorithms),* but most people have to look them up in books or online.

For a problem like this, a good algorithm to use is called a *binary search.* A binary search sounds complicated, but it's a simple idea. You put your first guess in the middle of all the possible numbers, and you ask your player whether the guess is high or low.

Now you have only half as many numbers to search through. That's a neat trick. So why not do it again? Split the remaining range in half and ask whether your guess is high or low.

Eventually the range shrinks to either two numbers or three numbers. If you have two numbers, you can check the higher one. If it is — boom! You're done. If not, it's one less.

If you have three numbers, you can check the middle number. If the guess is too low, you know it's the top number of the three. If not, you're down to two numbers and you can repeat the recipe from the previous paragraph.

You always guess the number, and you always do it in four or five tries. Figure 9-8 shows one example.

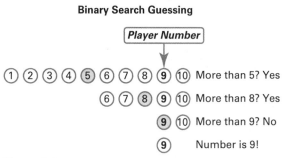

Binary Search Guessing

Figure 9-8

Can you write the code to improve the game with a binary search? There's a sample answer on the website for the book, but try to create your own answer first. Take as long as you need. If you get lost, try to break down the problem into simpler subproblems and work through them one by one.

The real magic comes from being able to guess much bigger numbers very quickly. Try to make your game guess numbers between 1 and 1,000. How many tries does it need? If you get it right, you'll find you need a lot less than 1,000. Or even 100.

Dig into Linux Commands

Linux is like an iceberg — not so much because it's big, cold, and it sinks ships (because it doesn't), but because the desktop you usually see is a small part of a much bigger thing.

To use the rest of the big Linux thing, you have to know how to type commands. You also need to find your way around all the files that make Linux work.

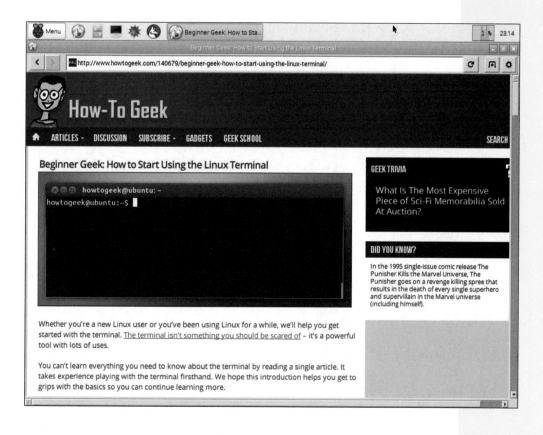

Understand the Command Line

Back in the days of computer prehistory, no one used a desktop because desktops hadn't been invented. Nor had mice. (Computer mice hadn't, anyway. Small furry mice that run around and squeak have been around much longer than computers have.)

There was only one way to use a computer: You had to type text commands with a keyboard. Want to see your files? Type a command. Want to start some software? Type another command. Want to shut down the computer so that both of you can get some sleep? There's a command for that.

In modern computers, this old system — called the *command line* — is still there, but it's hidden away. If you didn't know it was there, you'd never guess.

But it is. And you can do a lot more with it than you can using the desktop.

If you want to see pictures of old computers from the before-PC days, search the web for Computer Terminal. A very long time ago, computers could show only text, with no photos, videos, or game graphics. They printed the text on a huge reel of paper. The printer made a loud mechanical kerchunk as you typed each letter in a command. There would be a whole lot more kerchunking when the computer figured out and printed the result. Keeping a silent computer in your pocket is way less distracting.

Use Commands

When you type commands, you can't make spelling mistakes. You can't mix up capital letters with little letters because they mean different things. You have to get commands 100 percent right, or they don't work.

Computers are stupid. If you make a mistake the command line can't guess what you mean. It doesn't even try. It just says "Wut?" — only in more complicated computer-speak.

This need to be 100 percent super-accurate can make commands look like a hard way to do simple things. Viewing files and folders on the desktop is easy. The command-line makes it seem hard. The same is true for editing and for almost everything you're used to doing with a computer.

But there *is* an important upside. If you have serious hacker skills, you can chain commands together to do useful things. For example, you can rename all the files in a folder without typing the new names by hand. Or you can find all the files of a certain type, like photos or MP3s, and move them all to one folder from all over your computer. Or you can set up the command system so that it runs commands every hour, every day, every week, or every month.

Don't think of commands as a hard way to do simple things. Think of them as building blocks you can glue together to make your own smarter commands.

Put simply, you can use commands to customize your computer so that it works harder for you, does the stuff you want more quickly, and serves you better.

Get Started with Commands

When your Pi is ready for commands it displays a *prompt* — a dollar sign ($) at the end of some gobbledeegook. When you power up your Pi, the first thing you see after it settles down is this dollar prompt.

Any time you type startx to make the desktop appear, you are using the command-line. You just didn't know it!

Commands are so useful, you can use them on the desktop. A special application called LXTerminal shows the command line. Figure 10-1 shows LXTerminal doing the big Linux thing.

If you have an old-style desktop, launch LXTerminal by double-clicking the LXTerminal icon.

On the new desktop, click the LXTerminal icon once. It looks like a monitor with a black window in the icon bar at the top of your screen.

After it launches, you see a tab with the current prompt, like the one in Figure 10-1. Type commands after the prompt, and your Pi does what you tell it to.

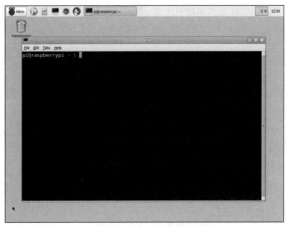

Figure 10-1

The prompt doesn't just listen and wait. It tells you useful stuff. The first part shows you your username and the name of the computer, which is raspberrypi, in case you've forgotten. The rest shows you the current working directory/folder.

The figures in this project show Terminal set up with extra-big letters to make it easy for you to read commands. When you use Terminal on your Pi, the letters will be smaller. You can change them by choosing Edit⇨Preferences and selecting a different font size.

Understand magic word commands

Linux includes hundreds of commands. No one remembers them all!

Unfortunately, most of the commands don't look like English. You can't guess them, no matter how good you are with computers.

Some people think commands are like magic words. You have to know the right words to make a command work.

Because you can't guess commands, you have to find them online or learn them from someone who already knows them. Be prepared to spend time online looking up commands and finding "magic word" examples that do what you want.

Don't search online for "magic word commands" because you won't find anything useful. Grown-up computer users don't like calling them magic word commands — even though that's what they are.

Use switches

Many commands include options called *switches*. Switches change what a command does.

To include a switch, you usually type a minus sign - after a command, followed by one or more letters or numbers. (Some switches use two minus signs –, but that's not so common.)

Figure 10-2 shows an example of using the `ls` command with different switches. `ls` lists the files in a folder. If you use it without switches, you get a list of the files and no other information.

Commands can have lots and lots of different switches. Only a few are really useful. The rest are there because someone decided it would be a good idea to include them — but they're not used much.

If you add the -l switch (type `ls -l` and press Enter), the command shows the size, date, and time the file was created, and who created it, for every file.

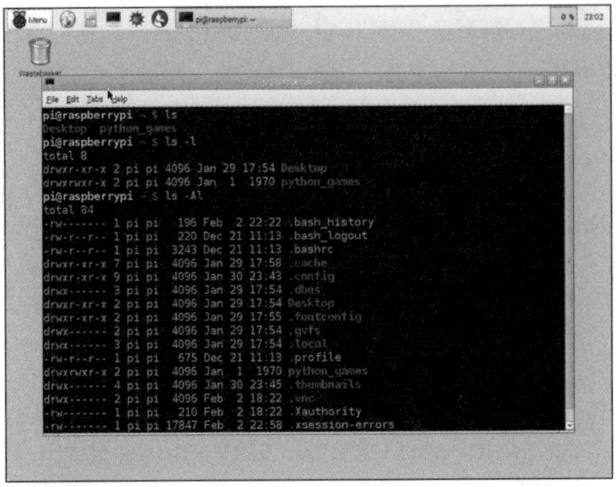

Figure 10-2

If you add the -A switch (type `ls  -A` and press), you get a list of invisible files.

For some commands only, you can combine switches to save typing. So `ls  -Al` works and shows you all the hidden files, with all their details.

Invisible files? Huh? Your operating system has been lying to you! But the files aren't really invisible. They just don't show up unless you look for them. They include settings for apps, settings that control what happens when you log in to your Pi, and other stuff you probably don't want to look at all the time. Hiding them helps avoid clutter. So leaving them invisible makes sense. Sort of. . . .

Find and Learn Commands

Because you can't guess commands and switches, you have to know how to find them. If you use the command line a lot, you'll learn the most useful commands by heart without really trying to.

A lot of people write out a cheat sheet to help them learn commands and switches. Unless you have the best memory in the history of the universe, you'll probably forget some of the commands and switches on your sheet. This is normal, so it's handy to have a list to remind you.

You can find the most useful commands online. Figure 10-3 shows one of the many sites that list popular Linux commands, with some of their switches.

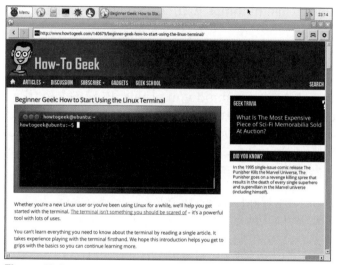

Figure 10-3

 In theory, you can use a Linux command called man to find out more about a command. When you type man [commandname] and Enter, you'll see lots of details. Helpful? Not really. man is great for experts. It's not designed for beginners. The help is extremely technical, so it's very hard to understand. And it doesn't list switches in order of usefulness. Obscure switches no one uses get equal billing with essential switches that are really useful. So it's best to ignore man and look for help online.

Play with cd and ls

To get started with commands, play with two — cd, and ls.

ls is short for — who knows? List something? Lively snowbunnies? Letter soup? It's a classic magic word command. It looks a bit like list files, but you'd never guess unless someone told you.

cd is short for change directory. You can use it to explore the directories (folders) in your Pi. When you type cd and a directory name, you move to that directory. (Technically, you set the working directory.) You can now list files, copy files, delete files, and generally do useful things without having to type the directory path again.

Directory and folder mean the same thing. When you look at files on the desktop, they're collected into folders. There's even a small folder icon to remind you of this. But back in the days of computer prehistory, these folders used to be called directories. They're two ways to look at the same thing. One way has a pretty picture, and the other has text commands. But both work on the same files. Two views. One thing. K?

You've already tried ls, so you know what's in your home pi directory. But what other files live inside your Pi?

Type cd / and press Enter. Now you're in the Pi's top directory. It holds all the files in your Pi. Type ls and Enter. You should see the list of directories shown in Figure 10-4.

Figure 10-4

If you've read Chapter 5, you'll know that files are organized in a big upside-down tree, with the / directory at the top, and lots of other directories inside it. The directories keep branching out and down for a good few levels.

You also know that every file and folder has a unique path, so you can find it. (If you haven't read Chapter 5 yet, you may want to read it now because it explains this stuff in detail.)

You can use cd to move to any directory by typing its path after the command. Unlike File Manager, it won't show you all the other directories you could be in. But the idea is sort-of similar-ish, kind of, if you squint and scrunch up your face and don't think about it too hard.

For example, cd /home/pi takes you back to the pi user directory.

You have to press Enter after every command. This tells your Pi to stop waiting and do what you want. You've probably figured this out now, so for now, just assume that you need to press Enter at the end of every command to make it work.

Learn more about cd

Typing full paths wastes time, so cd includes some shortcuts you can use. You can use these shortcuts and the full command with a path to cd to any directory in your Pi. Table 10-1 summarizes the shortcuts.

Here's an even faster shortcut. You can use ls and a path to list the files in a directory without cd-ing to it first. So why use cd? Because if you want to copy, move, or rename files in a directory, it's best to move there first with cd and save yourself some typing. Chapter 11 talks more about this.

Try cd a few times and see what happens. If you're paying attention, you see the prompt changes when you run it. The prompt shows you the current path! This is great — you don't have to remember where you are. The prompt always tells you.

Table 10-1	Using cd to Get Around
Command	**What It's For**
cd ~	Go to your home directory
cd /	Go to the top directory which holds all the others
cd directory	Go into a directory inside the current directory (only works if that directory exists)
cd ..	Go back up to the previous directory. (You can keep doing this until you get to /. The space before the dots is important!)
cd /path	Go straight to a directory when you know its path. (The / is important!)

To save space, some paths, like the home directory, use the short-cuts shown in Table 10-1. If you want to see a full path for the current directory, use a command called pwd — which is short for print working directory. It prints to the screen, and it doesn't make any kerchunk noises.

Meet Important Linux Directories

After you can use cd and ls (see previous section), you can go exploring. There's a lot to see, although much of it won't make sense yet.

Table 10-2 lists the most important directories at the top of the file tree. Linux is very organized, so there's a place for everything, and everything has a place.

You don't need to remember this list now — or maybe ever. But it's good to get an idea where everything goes. As you do more with your Pi, you'll be working inside some of these directories.

Table 10-2	What All Those Linux Directories Do
Directory	**What It's For**
/bin	Standard Linux system apps
/sbin	Standard Linux system apps for the superuser
/etc	Setup and configuration files (similar to preferences)
/var	Live information, including log files
/var/log	Log files left by running apps so that you can see what they've been doing and fix problems after something goes wrong
/var/www	After you set up a web server, files for web pages go here (before you set up a web server, this directory doesn't exist)
/home	All the home directories for every user (there's only one user on the Pi, so there's not much to see here)
/home/pi	The Pi user's home directory
/root	Files useful to the superuser (usually empty)
/usr	Files useful to all users
/usr/bin	Standard useful apps for all users
/usr/sbin	Standard apps for users pretending to be the superuser
/usr/local	Apps and other information that are only available on this computer and not on other Linux computers
/dev	Hardware settings (be careful!)
/lib	Software add-ons and special options
/proc	Information about apps that are running
/sys	Live hardware (be even more careful!)

Become a Superuser with sudo

You can't cd to some of these directories. If you try to, you get a message saying you don't have permission.

This isn't because you did a bad thing. It's because Linux is picky about security.

When you log into your Pi, you're an ordinary user. Linux doesn't trust ordinary users not to break things, so it locks you out of some directories.

Chapter 5 introduces the god-user or superuser, also known as root. The only way to look inside a protected directory is to make yourself root.

When you're using the command-line, you use a special command called sudo. To give yourself god-like superpowers, type sudo in front of a command. Linux assumes you're the god-user for that one command and lets you do whatever you like.

You can use sudo as many times as you want.

On some variants of Linux, sudo is sticky. You get superpowers for five minutes, and then you go back to being Mr. or Ms. Ordinary User. On the Pi, there's no stickiness. You have to type sudo before every superuser command. This is boring — yawn! — but if you type sudo su, you can make yourself root permanently. The prompt loses its colors to show you're in permanent god-mode. You stay in god-mode until you log out, or you use the exit command.

Serious grown-up Linux users don't like permanent god-mode. This is a smart thing on a big and serious grown-up computer with many users. It's not so important on a toy computer like the Pi, especially when you're the only user, and not being in god-mode makes it hard to get things done. Be careful about permanent god-mode — but not *too* careful.

Use Command Shortcuts

The command-line is picky about spelling, and it's easy to get commands wrong. Wouldn't it be useful if you could avoid retyping commands all the time?

You can. There are smart shortcuts that do exactly this.

Step back through commands

Press the up arrow key. You'll see the previous command you typed. Press it again. You'll see the command you typed before that, and so on, until you go back through every command you've ever typed.

If you want to run a command, press Enter in the usual way. Linux runs the command just as if you typed it by hand.

This is a super-useful shortcut. If you don't learn any of the others, learn this one!

Search for previous commands

Hold down Ctrl and R. Now type part of a command. Linux searches back through all the commands you've already typed and finds a match.

This option is less useful because sometimes the match isn't the one you want. But it's worth knowing that this option exists.

Use history

The history command shows a list of all previous commands. Figure 10-5 shows a short example.

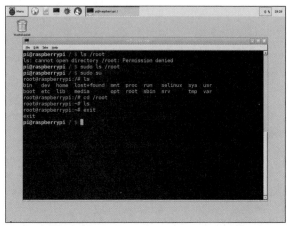

Figure 10-5

When you've been using your Pi for a while, the history list can get very long. To make it shorter, add a number. This number tells `history` to show only the last few commands. For example, `history 4` shows the last four commands.

But there's more! `history` shows a numbered list. You can rerun any command by typing ! followed by its number. (Don't include a space.) For example, `!12` reruns the 12th command in the list. This is an excellent way to avoid a lot of typing — and potential mistakes and retyping — when you want to repeat a long command you used a while back.

Manage and Customize Linux

All versions of Linux, including Raspbian, need more time and attention than a Mac or a PC. You'll find it's harder to install software, change preferences, and even to create and rename files in Linux.

You can automate some of the extra work by writing little mini-applications called scripts. You can also set up Linux so that it runs a command or script automatically at set times.

Even so, to really master Linux, you have to know a lot more about working with files than maybe you're used to.

Meet File Permissions

If you're used to a Mac or a PC, permissions can seem frustrating. They don't just work. You have to think about them all the time, even if you're doing something simple like making a file or folder.

There's no way around file permissions. You have to understand them and know how to use them, or you won't get much done with Linux.

Understand Read, Write, and Execute

In Linux, you can do three things to a file or folder: You can read it, you can change it, or you can run it as code.

These three permissions are called read, write, and execute. As you can maybe guess, you can set them separately for every file. For example, you can make a file read-only by turning off the write and execute permissions. Now you can't edit the file, and you can't run it as an app.

Why would you make a file read-only? For safety. Sometimes you want to protect a file so that you can't edit it.

Execute doesn't mean take it outside and shoot it. It means run it as code. No one knows why it's called execute and not run. At least it starts with a different letter than the other two options, so there's that.

In fact, Linux has three different permission settings for every file and folder:

✔ The owner of the file gets one set of permissions. Usually this set gives the owner permission to do anything with the files.

✔ The file's group (explained in the upcoming "Work with Users and Groups" section) gets another set. This set allows the file to be shared within a group.

✔ Everyone else gets yet another set. This set allows some files to be private, while others can be shared with everyone.

These different permission settings may seem super-complicated. Permissions were really designed for big computers with lots of users. On a big computer, it's useful to be able to hide some files from everyone else, to share others, and to make a few completely open.

On a computer like the Pi permissions make extra work for you. You're probably the only user, so it makes sense to be able to do anything to any file, doesn't it?

Not quite. In Linux, apps are users, too. You can use permissions to make sure that apps can't read or change files they don't need to.

Permissions get to be a big deal if you put your Pi on the Internet as a web server because it gives you some security from hackers.

Permissions also help keep you safe from mistakes because it's harder to delete important files by accident.

Check permissions

To check permissions on the desktop, open a Terminal window to show a command prompt. Then type the following command and press Enter:

```
ls -l
```

You see a list of files, with some extra letters at the left of the list. Figure 11-1 has an example. (You probably won't see the same files or the same permissions.)

The string of letters and dashes at the left of each item is a list of the permissions. They look like a row of ten letters:

```
drwxrwxrwx
```

If you see a letter, the permissions allow you to do that thing. If you see a dash, they don't.

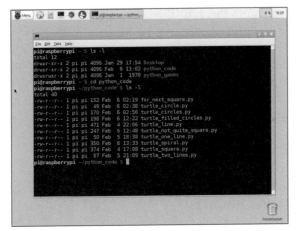

Figure 11-1

Most files have a lot of dashes, so you may see something like this:

```
-rwxrw-r---
```

Understand permissions

That row of letters isn't very easy to read, is it? It's like a code. But it's not a complicated code, and it's not very hard to understand it.

The first d is short for directory, which is another word for folder. If you see a d, it means that file is a folder/directory, and you can use the cd command to move inside and check whether it has any files.

The d isn't like the other letters. In fact, it's not really a permission. You can't change it. It appears in the row of letters because it's useful, but there was nowhere else to put it.

The next rwx is — you can maybe guess — the read, write, and execute permissions for the file.

Here's an example:

```
rw-
```

In English, the code means read: yes; write: yes; and execute: nope.

rwx — with dashes, if they're needed — appears three times on each row because there are three different sets of permissions.

In order, the first set of three lists permissions for the file owner.

The next set lists permissions for the file group.

And the last set lists permissions for everyone else — which means all the other users on the same computer.

Say that you want to work out what the following row of permissions means:

```
drwxrw-r--
```

You have to split it up into sets of three in your head, like this:

```
d rwx rw- r--
```

Then you can read the code for each set.

This is a folder/directory (d)

The file owner can read, write/edit, and execute (first three: rwx).

The group can read and write/edit only (second three: rw-).

Everyone else can only read the file (last three: r--).

Understand Users and Groups

What's a group? In Linux, every file and folder — every single one — is owned by a user. The owner is usually the user who created the file.

As the `pi` user, you own all the files you create in your home directory. Most of the other files are owned by `root`, the god-user. Giving them to the god-user protects them. It makes it harder for hackers to break into your Pi and harder for you to change or delete them by accident.

Wait — does that mean most of the files in your Pi don't belong to you? Yes. That is what it means. You're not the owner. As the `pi` user, you can't edit or execute a lot of files. That's why you have to use the `sudo` command to promote yourself to the god-user before you can change them.

Find out about groups

Files also belong to a *group*. A group is just a list of users. On big computers, groups help users work together. If you're part of a project group, you can share files with other members of the group, but keep them secret from everyone else.

On a small computer like the Pi, groups can have a single user. There's a pi group for the `pi` user and a root group for the `root` user. A lot of the time, you can ignore these group permissions.

But apps are users, too. They don't log in from the keyboard like you do, but they still have usernames and groups, and sometimes they own folders, too.

Groups are often used to share files between apps that work together. For example, all the apps that work with email can share files if they're part of the mail group. Some of the apps that keep your Pi running are part of a group called `staff`, which also includes the god-user.

You don't usually need to worry about these details. But sometimes you'll find that you have to change group permissions to get an app to run or to work with other apps.

Check users and groups

Figure 11-2 shows the files in one of the folders created for root — the god-user. You can see that two names appear after the permissions string. The first name is the file owner. The second name is the file group.

That's how you can check the owner and group of a file. Easy!

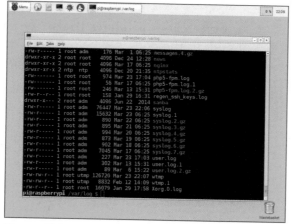

Figure 11-2

Understand everyone

You can use the final everyone permissions to control what other users can do with your files. Say that you have some pictures of kittens with rocket launchers you want to share with everyone. If you set the read permission in the everyone set of permissions, those kittens will be all over the network quicker than you can say viral.

If you want to hide the kittens, turn off the read permission for the everyone set, and they'll be hidden.

You also have to think about permissions when the pi user is in the everyone group. If you don't own a file or belong to the same group as the file, the everyone permissions set defines what *you* can do with it.

This is why you can't change files owned by root. As far as root knows, you're everyone. Most files owned by root don't have write permissions for everyone, so you can't edit them.

If the files don't have read permissions for everyone, you can't even read them

If this is a problem — it often is — you have to use the sudo command to promote yourself to the god-user before you can work with these files. As the god-user you become root, so now the files are yours.

Technically, the user permissions (not the everyone permissions) apply.

Work with Permissions

You need to know a handful of commands for working with permissions. Table 11-1 shows a list.

Table 11-1	Useful Permission Commands
Command	**What It Does**
ls -l	Lists files with permissions
chmod	Changes file permissions
chown	Changes the file owner
groups	Checks the users in a group
useradd	Adds a user to a group
chgrp	Changes the file group

You've seen how you can use the −l switch to check them when you use the ls command to list the files in a folder. But what if you want to change them?

Use chmod

To use chmod to change file permissions, you have to tell it three things:

- Who you're setting permissions for

- How you're setting them (there's more than one way . . .)

- What you're setting them to

An example command looks like this:

```
sudo chmod a+w filename-or-full-filepath
```

In the following sections, I break down this command. You have to start the command with sudo. Otherwise, you can't change permissions for files you don't have permissions for (if you see what I mean).

Select a who

Table 11-2 shows you how to pick a letter to tell the command who you're setting the permissions for.

Table 11-2	Who Am I Setting Permissions For?
Letter	What It Means
u	The owner of the file
g	The file group
o	Everyone who isn't the owner or the group
a	Everyone at all — no exceptions

Select a how

Next, you specify how you want to change the permissions. Table 11-3 has the details.

Table 11-3	How Am I Setting the Permissions?
Letter	What It Means
+	Adds/turns on a permission
-	Removes/turns off a permission
=	Ignores the current permissions and sets some new ones

The + and - options change the permissions that exist already. Use them if you want to add or remove a permission. For example, you can change the write permission only and leave the read and execute permissions alone.

The = option changes all the permissions at once. Use it when you don't care about existing permissions, and you just want to swoop in and set them all how you want.

Select a what

Table 11-4 shows you which letters to type to select the different permissions. This part is easy. It looks a lot like the "Understand Permissions" section.

Table 11-4	What Am I Setting?
Letter	Read r
r	Read permission
w	Write permission
x	Execute permission
X	Special magic execute permission for folders

Most of these do what you expect, but execute has some special features:

✔ You can look inside a folder only if you can execute it. You may think read would be enough, but it isn't.

✔ You can rename a file only if you can execute it. You may think write would be enough, but it isn't.

✔ As long as you can read a file, you can run it as code if it gets passed to some other app. You may think you need execute, but you don't.

For example, if you have permission to read a file, you can run it as Python code because you're actually executing Python first. Python reads the file, so it's Python's permissions that matter.

You need the execute permission only if the file is a self-contained app.

Confused? Probably. There's no simple way to make sense of these special cases. You just have to think them through, remember them, and say "Huh" a lot when you forget them, until you check online and remind yourself.

If you're trying to make software work together — for example, if you're trying to use Python to create a web page for you — and you're getting nothing, it's a good bet the permissions aren't right.

Sometimes permissions *fail silently.* Nothing appears on the screen. Stuff just doesn't work, and you have no idea why. As a rule, when something doesn't work and you have no idea, check the permissions first.

Put it all together

Permissions are complicated, so you need to practice them. You probably won't remember them otherwise.

Here's a simple example. Say that you want to set permissions so that everyone who uses our Pi can write a file. Can you work out what the command should be? Assume that everyone can read it already.

It should look like this:

```
sudo chmod a+w filename-or-full-filepath
```

Figure 11-3 shows a before-and-after so that you can see how this command changes the permissions string when you use the ls command. After the command, everyone can edit the file.

If you want to set multiple permissions, put them together like this:

```
sudo chmod a+rwx filename-or-full-filepath
```

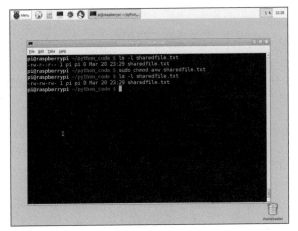

Figure 11-3

 You don't need to use sudo to change the permissions on the files you own, so you can usually do whatever you like to files in your home directory. But if you're trying to work with files elsewhere in your Pi, you definitely need sudo.

Use numbers

Sometimes permissions look like numbers. For example, blog articles and books sometimes tell you to set the permissions on a file to 777 or 644 or some other number.

Numbers are just a quicker and more compact way to define permissions. They're easier to remember than a long row of letters. They're also quicker to type.

But what do they mean? The first number sets your personal permission, the second number is the group permission, and the third number is the everyone else permission. So this is really just another way to write `rwx` three times.

Table 11-5 shows you how to convert between a three-letter permission string into a single number.

Table 11-5	Permissions as Numbers		
Number	**Read r**	**Write w**	**Execute x**
7	r	w	x
6	r	w	-
5	r	-	x
4	r	-	-
3	-	w	x
2	-	w	-
1	-	-	x
0	-	-	-

Some examples:

```
744 = rwxr--r--
777 = rwxrwxrwx
600 = rw-------
```

You can use the numbers instead of the letters in `chmod`, like this:

```
sudo chmod 644 filename-or-full-filepath
```

This sets the permissions to

```
rw-r--r—
```

Use the −R switch

If you want to change all the permissions inside a directory, you can change them for every file by hand — which can take a very long time.

Save yourself the effort with the −R switch. You can use it to change all the permissions for all the files inside a folder with a single command. To use it, include −R somewhere in the command when you type it.

Work with Users and Groups

To use permissions, you also need to know how to work with users and groups using the chown and chgrp commands.

The chown command changes the owner and/or the group of a file. You have to run it with sudo, like this:

```
sudo chown new_owner:new_group file_or_path
```

You can include a new owner before the colon, or a new group after the colon, or both.

So if you wanted to hand a file to root, the command would be

```
sudo chown root:root file_or_path
```

There's only one g in chgrp.

Use groups

The groups command shows the groups a user belongs to. If you just type groups on its own, it shows the groups *you* belong to, as the pi user.

Figure 11-4 shows the groups for pi and for root. Surprise! The pi user belongs to a lot of groups.

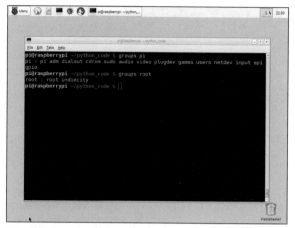

Figure 11-4

Belonging to these groups ensures that when you log in as the `pi` user, you can use some of the Pi's built-in software without having to join the groups first. This is important for video and audio. If the `pi` user didn't belong to the video and audio groups, you wouldn't be able to use a camera or get sound out of the headphone jack.

Add users to groups

You can use the `useradd` command to add a user to a group, like this:

```
sudo useradd -G groupname username
```

The `-G` switch is important. The group name always follows it. You usually need to include the `sudo`.

You won't usually need to make a new group. But if you do, you can use the `groupadd` command, like this:

```
sudo groupadd newgroupname
```

For new groups, you have to include `sudo`.

Make and Work with Files

After you know how permissions work, you can start making and managing files. If you don't understand permissions, you'll get a lot of `permission denied` error messages whenever you try to do something outside your home directory.

If you know how permissions work, you know how to get around this issue.

Using the desktop File Manager won't fix permission problems, so the File Manager is actually kind of useless. You typically have to fix permissions using Terminal and the command line before you can make and/or edit files on the desktop, especially if they're the files used for important Linux settings.

Create a file

To make a file, use the `touch` command, like this:

```
touch new-file-name
```

For example:

```
touch mynewfile.txt
```

If you're working in your home directory, `touch` makes a file that belongs to the pi user and the pi group with permissions that look like this:

```
-rw-r--r--
```

You can edit this file, but you can't execute it directly as an app. Other users can read it but not change it.

Files include a last time you did something to it time and date memory. If you `touch` a file that already exists, that time/date gets updated.

Create a file as root

If you're digging around inside the guts of Linux, you usually have to make a file as root. The command is

```
sudo touch new-file-name
```

This command makes a file owned by root and a member of the root group. The permissions are still

```
-rw-r--r--
```

But these permissions mean only the root user can edit the file!

If you try to edit it as the `pi` user, you get a `permission denied` message. (Remember, only the last `r---` applies to the `pi` user, so you can read the new file, but not write to it.)

Permission problems like this one are often inconvenient, unhelpful, irritating, distracting, frustrating, and generally not good.

So unless there's some super-important hacker-proof reason not to, you need to change the permissions so that you can edit the file as pi, like this:

```
sudo chmod a+w new-file-name
```

Now you can edit the file as `pi`. Editing the file is more useful than it looks because it means you can edit the file from the desktop using the Leaf editor.

Copy files and directories

To copy a file, use the `cp` command, like this:

```
cp old-file-name-or-path new-file-name-or-path
```

If you're working in your home directory, copying just works. You can use file names only, and you don't have to think about paths.

What about permissions? Copying a file creates a new file with the contents of the old file. (What else would cp do?)

But you're the owner of the new file, and it has the usual permissions:

```
-rw-r--r--
```

So if you copy a file owned by root, you can edit the copy. This process isn't always useful, but it's worth knowing.

To copy a file to a different directory, you have to have write permission for that directory.

Rename files and directories

To rename a file, use the mv command, like this:

```
mv old_file_name new_file_name
```

mv is actually short for move, so you can also use it to move a file to another directory:

```
mv file_name directory_path
```

Delete files and directories

The easy way to delete a file is to use the rm command, like this:

```
rm file-name
```

You need write permission for the file. If you don't have it, you can force the command to work with sudo.

To remove a directory, use the -r switch. (-R works too.)

```
rm -r directory-name
```

This command deletes the directory and everything inside it, including all directories.

Linux is picky about deleting directories if they're not empty. You can make it less picky with the -f switch, like this:

```
sudo rm -rf directory-name
```

This command will nuke the directory from orbit. Everything inside it, including all the directories, will disappear, forever. Linux won't ask you to confirm.

Obviously, you only want to use this command if you're really, really sure you know what you're doing.

Use wildcards

Often you want to work with all the files in a directory at once. To help with this need, Linux has a special feature called a *wildcard*.

To delete all the files in the current directory, type an asterisk for the filename, like this:

```
rm *
```

You can also add a file extension. For example, to delete all the files with .py extension — the ones with Python code — type this:

```
rm *.py
```

And you can pick all the files in another directory by adding the path before the wildcard:

```
rm /home/someotheruser/*.py
```

Wildcards also work when copying.

Install Software

As you've guessed now, in Linux, basic file operations are not completely simple. So you may think that installing software is even harder.

It's not! Or rather it is, but Linux makes it easy for you.

Linux uses a tool called a *package manager* to install software. A lot of software relies on other software, and you have to install all of it to get something working. The complete blob of everything that gets downloaded when you install software is called a *package*.

When software needs other software to work, the second software is called a *dependency*.

In Raspbian and Debian, the package manager command is apt-get. It works like this:

```
sudo apt-get install package-name
```

You get the package name by looking online. Often someone tells you the name.

apt-get often asks you yes/no to confirm that you want to go ahead. You can skip this step by including the -y switch:

```
sudo apt-get install -y package-name
```

As apt-get works, you see a lot of messages scrolling by. You can ignore them all.

One thing you can't ignore is the Internet. apt-get only works if your Pi has an Internet connection.

The other one thing you can't ignore is sudo. You have to include it when you install software — always.

Update and upgrade

Although Linux gets packages from the Internet, it keeps a list of dependencies on your Pi. Packages change all the time as the developers who put them together add new options and fix problems.

To make sure all dependencies are up to date, run

```
sudo apt-get update
```

before you install anything. You won't break anything if you don't, but it's a good idea to work with a fresh package list.

If you want to get the very latest versions of software you installed already, run

```
sudo apt-get upgrade
```

This command upgrades all the software on your Pi to the latest version. It can take a while to run, so you don't need to do it often. Figure 11-5 shows one example output. You have to press Y and Enter to confirm.

Figure 11-5

Uninstall software

You don't often need to uninstall software on a Pi. You won't usually run out of space on your memory card.

But just in case you do, you can use either of two commands:

```
sudo apt-get remove package-name

sudo apt-get purge package-name
```

Remove deletes the software. Purge deletes the software and all its settings — which is useful if you mess up the settings and you need to start again.

Week 4
Fun Pi Software Projects

In this part, you'll . . .

Don't forget to check out the online articles and bonus chapters at www.dummies.com/extras/ raspberrypiforkids.

Throw Shapes with Turtles

# CHAPTER 12

Python includes a turtle. It's not a real turtle, because you'd have to feed it and look after it — which would be cute, but probably wouldn't teach you much about computers.

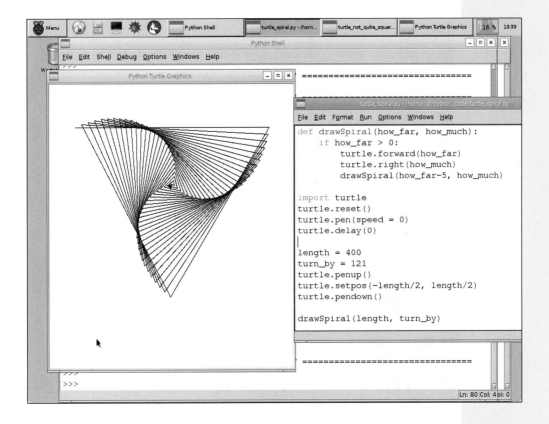

Meet the Python Turtle

The Python turtle is a drawing bot. You can steer it around the screen and make it draw shapes. With only a little programming magic, you can make awesome pictures that will make your friends believe you're a computer genius.

On the Raspberry Pi, the turtle is built right into Python. To use it, add a single line to the start of your code, like this:

```
import turtle
```

That's all you need. You can now write commands for the turtle. When you run your code, the turtle appears in a special window. It draws a line as it moves. It's that simple!

Figure 12-1 shows the turtle drawing a complicated shape using a few simple commands.

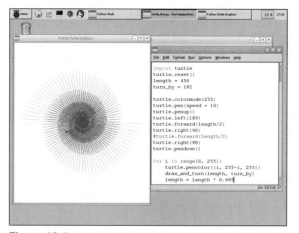

Figure 12-1

Get started with turtle commands

Turtle programming is really, really easy because there are only three kinds of commands:

> ✔ The first kind turns the turtle.

> ✔ The second kind moves it and draws a line.

> ✔ The third kind turns drawing on and off, changes the pen color, and does other useful stuff, like clear the screen.

Most turtle programs have a block of starting code to set up the turtle and maybe define useful numbers and shapes. Then there's another block of code to move the turtle and make the drawing appear.

That doesn't sound hard, does it? It isn't!

Get ready

You have to import the turtle before it works. It's also useful to reset the turtle before you start drawing. You don't *really* need to reset the turtle in Python, but it's good to get into a habit of making sure that the turtle is in the middle of the screen whenever you draw anything.

When you add a reset command, your startup code looks like this:

```
import turtle
turtle.reset()
```

Draw a line

Figure 12-2 shows how to draw a line. The turtle starts out in the middle of the window, facing right. To move it forward, add

```
turtle.forward(200)
```

Why 200? Why not? The bigger the number, the longer the line. Try drawing lines with smaller and bigger numbers and see what happens.

Figure 12-2

If you make a line too long, the turtle drives past the edge of the window. It still responds to commands, but you can't see it unless you move it back inside the window.

The turtle doesn't have to move forward. You can use a minus (negative) number to make the turtle go backwards! The `turtle.backward()` command does the same thing:

```
turtle.forward(-200)
turtle.backward(200)
# Both commands do the same thing
```

Why have both? Because sometimes you want to use math to work out how far the turtle should move. It's easier to use `turtle.forward()` for everything, with a negative distance when that's what your drawing needs.

Turn

Turning is just as easy as drawing a line. But you need to know how far to turn. The turtle can turn a complete circle. Turns are measured in *degrees,* and there are 360 degrees in a circle.

Figure 12-3 shows how turning works. When you turn, you have to imagine you're sitting on the turtle, or maybe walking on a big piece of paper pretending to be a turtle. Table 12-1 has a cheat sheet.

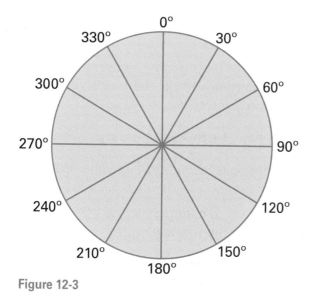

Figure 12-3

Table 12-1	Turtle Turning Table
Right Turn	**New Direction**
0	Straight ahead — no change
90	Hard right
180	A complete 180, so facing behind you
270	Hard left
360	Same as 0

To turn, use the right or left turn commands, like this:

```
turtle.right(90) # turn hard right
turtle.left(90)  # turn hard left
```

You don't have to turn in multiples of 90. You can turn by any number from 0 to 360, but multiples of 90 are easy to understand. You may have to think a bit harder to work out what a 175 degree turn does, but sometimes the only way to make a picture is to use weird turn values.

Understand left and right

Turtle directions are like driving directions, not map directions. In a car, grown-ups usually say, "Take the next right, then the second left, and then carry on for a block."

They don't usually say, "Head west, then north, and then. . . ."

This is why in turtle-speak `right(90)` means turn right. It doesn't mean face east.

But what about turning left? If you turn left, you get a mirror of Table 12-1. Turning right 270 degrees leaves your turtle facing the same direction as turning left by 90 degrees. (If you can't see why, try it with your turtle.)

Sometimes it's simpler to do right turns all the way. Other times it's simpler to turn left for some turns and right for others.

It's up to you to turn your turtle whatever way works for you.

Draw another line

You can turn your turtle as much as you want. It never gets dizzy or bored. But spinning it around forever won't help you make cool drawings.

To draw a new line, use forward or backward, just as you did to make one line.

If you don't turn the turtle or turn it by 0, the new line goes on the end of the old line to make one long line.

If you turn the turtle, you get a line at an angle to the original line. Figure 12-4 shows what happens when you tell your turtle to go forward, turn by 90, and go forward again. Here's the code:

```
turtle.forward(200)    # draw a line
turtle.right(90)       # turn hard right
turtle.forward(200)    # draw another line
```

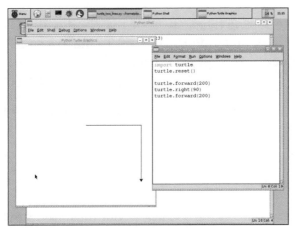

Figure 12-4

TIP

If you're lazy, you can save typing with shortcuts — fd for forward, bk for back, rt for right, and lt for left.

Draw and Move

To make shapes, draw lots of lines. It's easy to make stars, squares, triangles, and other simple shapes by moving and turning over and over.

Draw a square

You can draw a square by moving and turning four times, like this:

```
turtle.forward(200)    # draw a line
turtle.right(90)        # turn hard right
turtle.forward(200)    # draw a line
```

```
turtle.right(90)        # turn hard right
turtle.forward(200)     # draw a line
turtle.right(90)        # turn hard right
turtle.forward(200)     # draw a line
turtle.right(90)        # turn hard right
```

This puts the turtle back where it started, facing in the direction it started.

It works, but repeating the same code over and over isn't very neat. It's a lot of typing. And if you want to make a smaller square, you have to change the length of each side separately — which is a lot of work.

You can save yourself some typing with a for loop, like this:

```
for turns in range (0, 4):
    turtle.forward(200)
    turtle.right(90)
```

Figure 12-5 shows the result. Now you can make the square bigger or smaller by changing one number.

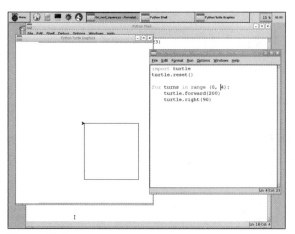

Figure 12-5

You can also mirror the square by changing the right(90) to a left(90). What happens? Can you guess?

As usual with Python, `range(0, 4)` means 0..3 and not 0..4. You get four sides of a square because you start counting from 0.

Work out where the turtle is

When you draw with a computer, you need to know where you are on the screen. Turtle instructions — left, left again, right, and so on — work well for simple drawings, but after you've drawn a couple of lines it's hard to work out where you are or where you're heading.

Computers treat windows and screens as a grid of dots. To pick a dot, you use two numbers. You count across from left to right. Then you count up from the bottom of the screen or window.

The left/right count is called the *x coordinate*. The up/down count is called the *y coordinate*. Coordinates often appear in brackets, like this:

```
(200, -100)  # (x, y coordinates, in order)
```

One dot is special. It's called the *origin*. When you count, you count from the origin.

Sometimes the origin is at the top left of the screen or window. Sometimes it's at the bottom left.

For the turtle, the origin is right in the middle of the drawing window, which makes counting a little more complicated. To work out where you are, you count down from the bottom or left with a minus sign in front of the coordinate, until you hit the origin. Then you start counting up again.

Figure 12-6 is a handy guide to working out where you are in Turtle Space. If it looks too math-y and scary and makes you feel like you want to hide under the bed until it goes away, Table 12-2 says the same thing in a different way.

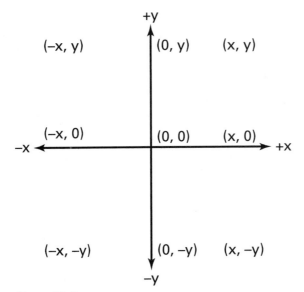

Figure 12-6

Table 12-2	Counting and Moving in Turtle Space
Where Am I?	**How Do I Know?**
Left of the middle	-x, counting down as you move left
Right of the middle	x, counting up as you move left
Below the middle	-y, counting down as you move up
Above the middle	y, counting up as you move up

Move in the window

You can use the *(x, y)* numbers to park the turtle anywhere on the screen. The setposition command — you can shorten it to setpos or use goto instead — moves the turtle to any *(x, y)* position.

```
turtle.setposition(100, -100)
turtle.setpos(100, -100)
turtle.goto(100, 100)
```

```
# These all do the same thing
```

 If the moving around thing still doesn't make sense, drive the turtle to various *x, y* positions until it does. Python is great for just playing around. If you get lost, use `turtle.home()` to move the turtle to the middle of the screen.

If you want the turtle to move in the *x* or the *y* direction only, there's a command for that:

```
turtle.setx(somenumber)
# Move the turtle left or right only

turtle.sety(somenumber)
# Move the turtle up and down only
```

You can find out where you are. These examples print the values, but you can also use them to move the turtle by some by reading *x* and/or *y*, changing them with some math, and using `setx` and `sety` to move the turtle to its new home.

```
print turtle.xcor()      # Show the x coordinate
print turtle.ycor()      # Show the y coordinate
print turtle.position() # Show (x, y)
```

Turn to a heading

What about turning? You can use `setheading()` to set the turtle direction using map directions, not turtle directions.

`setheading()` doesn't care where the turtle is facing before the command. After the command, it always faces the direction you set.

Table 12-3 has a cheat sheet. You don't have to use multiples of 90 — not unless you're drawing a lot of squares, anyway.

Table 12-3	Using setheading()
New Heading	**Makes the Turtle Point . . .**
0	Right
90	Down
180	Left
270	Up

Draw a circle

You can probably guess this one. To draw a circle, use

```
turtle.circle(somenumber)
```

somenumber sets how big the circle is.

Technically, somenumber sets the radius — the distance between the middle of the circle and the edge. A circle is always twice as wide as its radius. (You don't need to remember any of this until you're in high school.)

You can draw an arc by adding another number, which sets how far around the circle goes in degrees. A full circle is 360 degrees. A half circle is 180 degrees. A quarter circle is 90 degrees and so on.

```
turtle.circle(somenumber, arc)
```

circle() draws in the wrong direction! You probably expect the turtle to make a circle by turning right because that's the way the hands on a clock go around. But it turns left, which is weird, unexpected, strange, and *just wrong*.

Control the Pen

Sometimes you want to make a drawing with lots of different shapes. The turtle usually draws a line when you move it. To move it without drawing, use the penup() command, like this:

```
turtle.penup()      # Stop drawing
# Add code to move the turtle here
turtle.pendown()    # Start drawing again
```

Use these commands to move the turtle to a new starting point when you start a new shape, without trailing an ugly line behind it.

Change the speed

The turtle moves slowly so that you can see what it's doing. This works fine for simple shapes. But as you draw more complicated shapes, waiting for the turtle to finish can get boring.

You can make the turtle speed up with a couple of extra lines:

```
turtle.pen(speed = 0)
turtle.delay(0)
```

The pen speed sets how fast the turtle moves. 1 is slow, 10 is fast. 0 is instant, which probably isn't what you expected, but there it is.

For even more speed boost, set the turtle delay to 0. The Pi isn't a fast computer, so it still takes a few minutes to draw a complicated shape.

You can also slow down the turtle with a smaller pen speed. You may want to check what the turtle is doing. It's easier to see when it's not moving so fast.

 As the turtle moves around, Python updates the screen and then waits a while. `turtle.delay` sets the wait time. When the delay is 0, Python doesn't wait at all, which makes the turtle go faster.

Understand colors

Drawing software often makes colors by mixing red, green, and blue. You pick a color by telling the computer how much of each color you want. The color recipe looks like three numbers in a row with commas between them:

```
(1, 0, 0) # This makes red
(0, 1, 0) # Green
(0, 0, 1) # Blue
```

You can mix all of the colors to make more colors:

```
(1, 1, 1) # White
(0, 0, 0) # Black
(1, 1, 0) # Yellow
(1, 0, 1) # Pinky purple
(0, 1, 1) # Light Blue
```

That mix of green and blue has a special name — *cyan,* pronounced sigh-ann. It's used a lot in science-fiction films whenever the director wants to make something look technological and science-y.

That gives you eight colors, which is a good start. But what if you want gray instead of white or black?

You don't have to use whole numbers. You can use decimals instead:

```
0.5, 0.5, 0.5    # Medium gray
0.25, 0.25, 0.25 # Dark gray
0.75, 0.75, 0.75 # Light gray
```

Of course, you can use different decimals to make any color mix. There are so many colors, they don't all have names:

```
0.1, 0.2, 0.5    # Not quite deep blue
```

Understand color modes

Decimals aren't easy to use. If you want less obvious fractions, you have to do a lot of typing:

```
0.3333333, 0.3333333, 0.3333333 ; 33% gray
```

And decimals are really a cheat. You may think there's a difference between 0.3333333 and 0.3333334. But there isn't because most computers give you only 256 brightness steps for each color.

This isn't as a bad as it sounds. With 256 steps for each color, you still have more than 16 million colors altogether (256 x 256 x 256). That's more than your eyes can see, so it should be enough.

With the Python turtle, you can choose how you want to mix colors by setting the `colormode` option. You need to set it only once at the start of your code, and it sticks for all the colors you make after that:

```
turtle.colormode(1)
# Make colors with decimals between 0 and 1

turtle.colormode(255)
# Make colors with whole numbers between 0 and 255
```

 Computers count from 0, which is why you use 255 and not 256. There are 256 steps because computers count in powers of 2, and 256 (2 x 2 x 2 x 2 x 2 x 2 x 2 x 2) is a convenient size for storing small amounts of information. It looks weird to humans, but you see it a lot in code.

Set the pen color

After you know how color modes work (see preceding section), you can make your turtle draw any color you want. The pen color setting is called . . . drum roll . . . `pencolor`. (Badish!) Figure 12-7 has an example:

```
turtle.colormode(255)
# You only need this line once


turtle.pencolor((50, 100, 150))
# Use this to change the RGB mix.
# Don't forget to include two brackets!
# You can change the color as often as you want
```

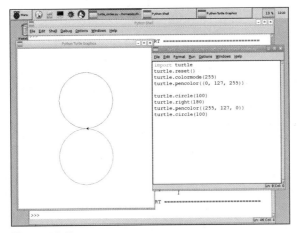

Figure 12-7

From then on, the turtle pen will draw with the new color. To change the color again, add another `pencolor` line.

Reset the pen and everything else, too

Lost and confused? Need to start again? Use

```
turtle.reset()
```

This command moves the turtle back to its starting position and direction.

Need to clear the screen and start a new drawing? Use

```
turtle.clear()
```

This command wipes the screen. But it doesn't move the turtle, so if you want to start from scratch add a `reset()`, too.

Draw with Functions

You can draw almost anything with a whole lot of move/turn commands. If you had a lot of patience and nothing else to do until you were 50, you could make your turtle copy famous art.

 But one of the cool things about computers is that you can do a lot with hardly any code. Here's a rule to remember: When you repeat code, there's always a way to make it simpler.

Simple code wins in four ways:

✔ Less typing

✔ Less thinking

✔ Fewer mistakes

✔ More possibilities

Code is a bit like building something with plastic blocks. But it's cleverer because when you make something once, you can reuse it. So once you write the code to draw a house, you can make copies of the house all over the screen.

How do you know what to repeat? Remember the rule! If you're writing the same code over and over, you can rewrite it as a ready-made block.

Python makes this easy. You copy the code you're repeating to a function. Then you can use it as a ready-made with a single line.

If you make a mistake, the mistake is in one place, so it's easy to fix it.

You can think of the function as a new command for your turtle. There's a huge win here. You can forget how the function works and just use it when you need it.

If you make a function to draw a house, you can draw houses all over the screen. You don't have to think about all the turning and drawing the turtle has to do. You can just say, "Draw me a house!" And it does.

Make a drawing function

Of course, you don't need to draw a house all the time. You can make functions do big, complicated things, or you can make them do small, simple things. As long as your function puts lots of repeated code in one place, it's going to help you.

For example, you can make a function to do something very simple — draw a line and turn the turtle. Because a lot of turtle code is draw/turn, it makes sense to put both commands together.

It's a good example because it's so simple. Here's the code:

```
def draw_and_turn(how_far, how_much)
    turtle.forward(how_far)
    turtle.right(how_much)
```

To use the code, fill in the numbers. You should see the same line you saw in Figure 12-2

```
import turtle
turtle.reset()
draw_and_turn(200, 90)
```

Python functions go at the top of the window, before the rest of your Python code.

Use constants and variables

You can draw a square by repeating `draw_and_turn` four times, like this:

```
draw_and_turn(200, 90)
draw_and_turn(200, 90)
draw_and_turn(200, 90)
draw_and_turn(200, 90)
```

If you think about it, now you're repeating numbers instead of code. It would be a lot simpler to set the line length and turn length in one place. If you want to change them, you can edit one line instead of four.

If you're repeating something over and over, there's probably a neater way to write the code. Here's how to set the important numbers in one place:

```
length = 200
turn_angle = 90
draw_and_turn(length, turn_angle)
draw_and_turn(length, turn_angle)
draw_and_turn(length, turn_angle)
draw_and_turn(length, turn_angle)
```

Now you can change the length on one line to make your square bigger or smaller. That's a lot less typing than changing the length on every line.

You can even use a negative/minus length to make the turtle draw the square backwards. (What happens if you do?)

Repeat functions

In the example, the code repeats the function four times, which is not so great. Can you make it smaller? Yes, you can! You can use a `for` loop.

```
length = 200
turn_angle = 90
for i in range (0, 4):
  draw_and_turn(length, angle)
```

That's two lines saved, which isn't a big difference for a square.

Make awesome shapes with repeats

What if you make the angle more or less than 90 degrees? If you think about it, the square won't close. That's bad, right?

Maybe not. If you keep repeating the not-quite-square, the turtle keeps turning by a small amount and drawing lots of not-quite-squares, which looks kind of cool. Figure 12-8 shows what happens.

```
length = 200
turn_angle = 91
for i in range (0, 90):
  draw_and_turn(length, angle)
```

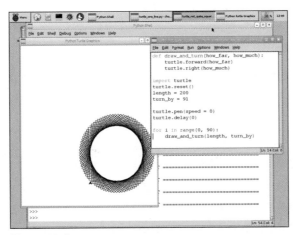

Figure 12-8

This is where repeats really pay off. Instead of writing draw_and_turn 90 times or separate draw and turn commands 180 times, your 4 four lines draw a complicated shape.

And you can make it even more complicated and interesting with more simple changes, like this:

```
for i in range (0, 90):
  draw_and_turn(length, angle)
  length = length * 0.99
```

This code makes the line just a tiny bit shorter on each repeat. It's a simple change, but it draws a much more interesting shape.

Try playing with this code and see what happens. Some things to try:

✔ Move the turtle before it starts drawing so that the shape is in the middle of the screen.

✔ Use the length variable instead of a number so that you can change the length and your shape stays centered.

✔ Change the pen color slightly for each repeat.

✔ Try different angles to see which ones make cool shapes.

Use Smart Repeats

In the code in the previous section, you have to guess how many repeats to set. It would be useful to have some way of stopping the repeats when the pattern looks good.

There's a neat way to do this. Instead of repeating a function in a loop, you can make a function repeat itself.

Huh? The code for a function can include the same function — like a snake biting its own tail, but without any YouTube videos showing how that works.

Meet recursion

You could call this repeat-a-repeat functionception, but no one is going to remember that movie ten years from now, and your parents probably didn't let you watch it anyway.

The official computer-speak name is *recursion.* It really just means making a thing do itself over and over until you tell it to stop.

Functions aren't like boxes. So recursion doesn't mean you're putting something inside another thing in a physical way you can't touch and that makes your brain go "Ow!" if you think about it.

It's easier to remember it as a cool way to do stuff over and over until you need to stop because you're done and can't do it anymore.

Use recursion

Adding recursion to a function is easy. You need two things:

✔ A way of telling the function to stop so that it doesn't go on for ever and force you to pull the plug on your Pi

✔ A repeat of the function inside the function

Sometimes you want to make some variable changes for the repeat. Sometimes you don't. It all depends.

Here's an example. It's based on draw_and_turn() with a couple of extra lines to add the Two Things You Need:

```
def draw_spiral(how_far, how_much)
if how_far > 0:
  turtle.forward(how_far)
  turtle.right(how_much)
  draw_spiral (how_far-5, how_much)
```

The first new line stops the function when the line gets so short it has nothing to draw. The second new line makes the function repeat itself to draw a slightly shorter line.

That's it. Figure 12-9 shows what you get when you set the angle to 121 degrees. The clever thing about the code is that it stops when it needs to. You don't need to tell it how many repeats to draw.

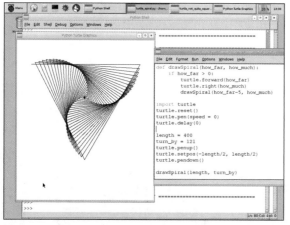

Figure 12-9

The other clever thing is that one line of code draws the whole spiral.

Recursion is a really good way to make complicated shapes, including ferns, trees, and fractals. There's some example tree code on the website for you to play with.

# CHAPTER 13

Combine Minecraft and Python

Minecraft is the world's most popular block mining game. Python is one of the world's most popular computer languages. How could they not go together?

Get Started with Minecraft

You can find the Pi edition of Minecraft in the Games heading of the main menu, as shown in Figure 13-1.

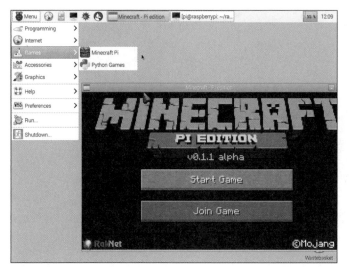

Figure 13-1

To use Minecraft:

1. **Launch the desktop with `startx` if it isn't already running.**

2. **Click the Menu button and choose Games and Minecraft Pi.**

   As Figure 13-1 shows, Minecraft launches in a small window and asks you to start a new game or join a game.

3. **Click Start Game, select world, and click Create New.**

   Minecraft shows a Generating world window as it makes a new world. This takes a while.

The Pi edition of Minecraft is very simple. It doesn't have most of the features of the full version, which include hell areas, dangerous chickens, witches, ocelots, slime, and flying pigs. For more on Minecraft's features, see http://minecraft.net.

Explore the World

The Minecraft world is made of blocks arranged in a 3D grid. Figure 13-2 is your first view of this new world.

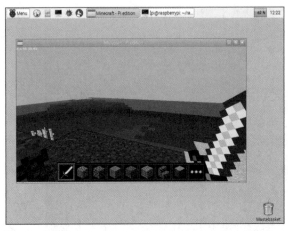

Figure 13-2

Drag the mouse to turn so that you can see different parts of the world. To move, press the keys listed in Table 13-1.

Table 13-1	Moving in Minecraft
Key	**New Direction**
W	Move forward
A	Shuffle left without turning
D	Shuffle right without turning
S	Move back
E	Show the blocks window
Esc after E	Hide the block window
Space	Jump once
Double-tap Space	If not flying, start to fly
	If flying, stop and fall
Tab	Release the mouse so you can use it on the desktop
Esc	Go to the game menu

Change the view

You may find it hard to use the default first-person view, which puts the camera in front of your player's eyes. It's kind of clumsy, and it's hard to see where you are.

To change the view, press Esc and click the second button at the top left of the window. When the icon changes to a rectangle with lines leading to a pair of blocks, click Back to Game.

Now the camera is behind your player. Some people prefer this view because it's easier to see what's happening.

Change the world

Minecraft is all about changing your world. To remove a block, click the left mouse button to swing your sword. After you hit a block a few times, it breaks into pieces and disappears.

It's hard to aim in Minecraft. You have to practice to work out which block your sword is going to hit.

If nothing happens when you left-click, move your player until a block is in front of you.

To build something new, press E to see all the blocks and other items you can use. Click one to select it. If it's a block and not a weapon, right-click to add it to the world. You can keep right-clicking, turning, and moving to add more and more blocks, as shown in Figure 13-3.

Figure 13-3

Understand APIs

In computerland, an *API* (application program interface) is a software control panel for a website, game, or other app. Instead of clicking a mouse and pressing keys to make things happen, you can send software commands using code. APIs can also tell you what's happening inside a website, game, or app.

APIs are everywhere. Twitter, Facebook, and other big websites have their own APIs.

As an example, here are a few things you can do with the Twitter API. This isn't the full list, but it does give you some hints:

🗸 **Make useful things happen automatically.** For example, you can use the Twitter API to send tweets automatically at set times. You don't have to be anywhere near a computer or phone to Tweet!

🗸 **Collect information.** For example, you can use the API to ask Twitter once a day how many followers you have and then draw a graph of the numbers.

✔ **Add smart new features.** Do you want to follow everyone who posts a word you're interested in, like the name of a band or a hot news topic? You can use the API to make it happen.

Understand the Minecraft API

The Minecraft API built into the Pi version is much simpler than the Twitter API, but you can still do some cool things with it. Here are some possibilities:

✔ Find out where your player is.

✔ Teleport your player to a new location.

✔ Build complicated shapes with blocks.

✔ Remove blocks with code — maybe to clear a big area.

Look at the Minecraft API

All APIs have a reference website with a list of commands — also known as *API calls,* or just calls for short.

The Minecraft API Reference is at `www.stuffaboutcode.com/p/ minecraft-api-reference.html`.

As shown in Figure 13-4, API reference pages often look complicated, but often that's because you get a list of calls and not quite enough explanation of what each call does, or how to use it, with examples.

The Minecraft API Reference has good examples, but the explanations are not very detailed. You have to do some guessing — which is normal when you're using an API.

Another missing feature is priority. All the calls get equal space, so you have no idea which calls are used a lot and which are hardly used at all.

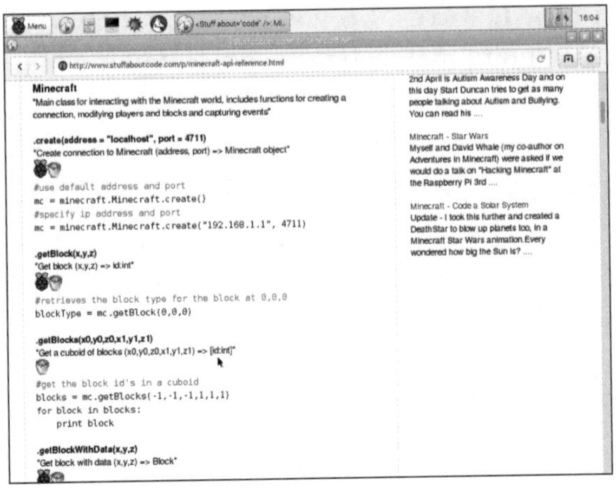

Figure 13-4

That's normal, too. It's up to you to decide which calls you want to use. It's a good idea to look through the list and copy/paste or make a note of calls that look interesting or useful. Then you can experiment with them. If you need to know more about them, you can look online for other examples.

Never try to learn all of an API before using it. You'd need a brain the size of a planet — which would make it hard to get out of bed in the morning — and a perfect memory. It's fine to keep looking stuff up. If you use an API a lot, you often learn the most useful calls without really trying.

Use the Minecraft API

Most projects that use an API start with *boilerplate* code that sets up the API so that you can use it later. For Minecraft, the boiler-plate code looks like this:

```
from mcpi import minecraft
mc = minecraft.Minecraft.create()
```

The code makes a variable called mc, which works like an invisible Minecraft control robot. When you send commands to mc, it passes them to Minecraft. Minecraft does the stuff you tell it to, or reports back with information you asked for, or both.

The API works by sending special messages to Minecraft — a bit like emails or texts. APIs are good at hiding details. They make it easy to concentrate on what you want to happen without worrying about technical details.

Use an API call

Here's a simple example showing how to use an API call:

1. **Choose Menu⇨Programming⇨Python 2 to launch the Python 2 editor.**

2. **Choose File⇨New Window to make a new file.**

3. **Type the following code:**

   ```
   from mcpi import minecraft
   mc = minecraft.Minecraft.create()
   x, y, z = mc.player.getPos()
   print x, y, z
   ```

   Can you guess what this does?

4. **Save the file as wherami.py.**

5. **Launch Minecraft if it's not already running.**

6. **Move around inside the game for a bit.**

7. **Then click the code window in the Python editor again and press F5 to run the code.**

8. **Move the player again and run the code again.**

   Figure 13-5 shows what you can get.

Figure 13-5

The code tells you where your player is in the Minecraft world! It uses three numbers. Table 13-2 shows you what they mean.

Table 13-2	Finding Yourself in Minecraft
Letter	What It Means
x	East/west on the grid
y	Up/down for flying and digging
z	North/south on the grid

There's no big arrow pointing north in Minecraft, so x and z are just for guidance. Even so, north is always in the same direction. It's not usually the direction you're facing.

Teleport in Minecraft

You can use a different API call to move around in Minecraft:

1. **Change the code so that it looks like this:**

```
from mcpi import minecraft
mc = minecraft.Minecraft.create()
```

```
x, y, z = mc.player.getPos()
mc.player.setPos(x, y + 100, z)
```

The `setPos()` API call moves your player to a new location.

2. **Move to another location, if you'd like.**

   You can do some basic math to the *x, y,* and *z* numbers to move from your current location to a new one. Or you can use some other numbers — maybe random numbers — to jump to some other place.

3. **Save the file as jump.py and press F5 to run it.**

   Figure 13-6 shows an example. The code makes you jump straight up by 100 grid blocks. If you're flying, you stay there. If you're not flying, you crash straight back down again.

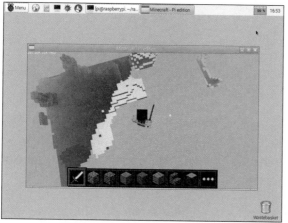

Figure 13-6

You don't die when you crash. Your player is made of *very* tough blocks.

Remove blocks

Hacking away at blocks with a sword is a really slow way to change the world. Is there a faster way?

If you look through the API, you won't find a `deleteBlock()` call, but there is a `setBlock()` call. It turns a block into a different kind of block.

Can you work out how to make blocks disappear now? You have to use a trick. In Minecraft, the entire world is made of blocks, across, left, right, up and down, in every direction, so there are no missing blocks.

The trick? Empty blocks are made of air. You can use `setBlock()` to turn stone and other blocks into air blocks to make them disappear.

Here's some code:

```
from mcpi import minecraft
from time import sleep

    mc = minecraft.Minecraft.create()
while True:
    x, y, z = mc.player.getPos()
    mc.setBlock(x, y - 1, z, 0)
    sleep (0.1)
```

The game is called Minecraft, so you can make a mine. The code removes the block your player is standing on. It loops forever, so it keeps removing blocks. The player falls into a bottomless shaft that gets deeper and deeper.

Save it as `death_dig.py` and run it. You may need to nudge your character into a hole to make the mineshaft appear. Eventually, you see the screen in Figure 13-7.

If you dig deep enough. Minecraft decides you've fallen out of the bottom of the earth and kills you.

Figure 13-7

TIP

The 0 at the end of the setBlock() call makes the block an air block. Minecraft has lots of different block types, and they all have a different number. If you scroll through the API reference, you can find a list of block types, with the number of each.

Make buildings

Of course, you can also take an air block and turn it into a stone or water block. Try the following:

```
from mcpi import minecraft
import random
mc = minecraft.Minecraft.create()

x, y, z = mc.player.getPos()
x = x + random.randint(-10, 10)
z = z + random.randint(-10, 10)
for i in range(0, 21):
    mc.setBlock(x, y + i, z, random.randint(1, 8))
```

Can you work out what this code does? The random.randint(a, b) calls produce a random — unpredictable — number between the first and second numbers in the brackets. For example,

```
random.randint(-10, 10)
```

makes a number between –10 and 10. You get a different number every time you run this code. It's supposed to be unpredictable, so you never know what you'll get.

Random code is a good way to add surprises. You can give the code an outline of something, and it fills in the details in surprising ways.

Here, the x and z positions are random so they stay close to the player, but not likely to be on top of the player.

Why does this matter? Because the rest of the code makes a simple building on the random position. It turns air blocks into other blocks.

The small 1, 8 range of randomness more or less guarantees that one of the blocks will be flowing water. Figure 13-8 shows what happens when you put everything together — you get a fountain!

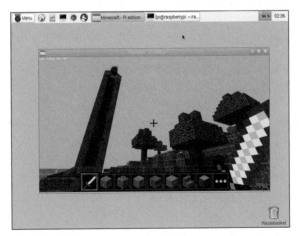

Figure 13-8

Minecraft makes the water pour off the fountain onto the ground, and into the sea. Because the blocks are random, the fountain is a little different every time you run the code.

Try a Few More Things

Here are some projects to try. As usual, some projects are harder than others. A few are very hard, but see how far you get with them anyway. You will need to research and learn more about Python to make some of them work.

- ✔ **Remove blocks as you walk.** This project is harder than it looks. How many layers of blocks do you need to get rid of before you can walk through the hole you make? How wide does the hole need to be? The easy option is to use lots of separate calls to `setBlock()`. Is there a neater way to make the code work with loops or conditionals?

- ✔ **Build bigger shapes.** Cubes and the like are easy. You can use a special API call for big square shapes with lots of blocks. But how about making a square, or a pyramid, or a grid of lines? If you have high school math, try making circles or spheres. Or try making a house.

- ✔ **Build a rocket.** Take the fountain/tower and make it fly into the sky. How do you keep the blocks together? Is there a simpler way to do it?

- ✔ **Make a firework.** At a certain height — say, 100 blocks — make all the blocks in the rocket explode in different directions. How can you keep track of the position of every block?

- ✔ **Build a maze.** This project is really hard to work out on your own, unless the maze is very simple. For help, see `http://en.wikipedia.org/wiki/Maze_generation_algorithm`. Try taking the Python code there and making it work in Minecraft. Make the walls so tall that your player is trapped inside them.

14

Make a Dumb Website

You can turn your Pi into a simple web server and use it to show simple web pages you can view in any web browser.

Meet Web Servers

A *web server* is a special kind of computer. Desktop and laptop computers can do lots of useful things. A web server does exactly one thing: It serves up web pages.

This maybe sounds wasteful. It isn't.

Big websites like Facebook (see Figure 14-1) have to serve a lot of pages quickly all through the day and night. It would be bad if Facebook slowed down whenever someone at Facebook HQ tried to play Minecraft. So if you're running a really big website, you put your web pages on a special server, and you set it up so that it doesn't do anything else.

Figure 14-1

You can't run all of Google or Facebook on your Pi because it isn't fast enough. (Really, it isn't.) Big sites have a lot of extra software custom-written for them. You can't install that software because it's not available to the public.

But you can still set up a simple web server that can handle maybe five or ten visitors at a time.

Understand Dumb Websites

A dumb website is just a file with a list of very simple instructions that define what appears on a web page. Most web content — the bits you can see — is words and letters, also known as *text*. Optionally, you can add pictures and YouTube links. Even more optionally, you can include animations, on-screen menus, and other clever things.

When you make a dumb website, the file of instructions for the browser changes only if you open it in a text editor and change it by hand. If you don't change anything, the site always shows the same words, pictures, and links. Often, this is called a *static website*.

Choose a Web Server

You can install a web server on your Pi in the usual way with `apt-get`. Because this is Linux, you get a choice of servers. Table 14-1 shows the list.

In this project, you install a server called nginx (engine x) because it's a good server, and it's easy to get it working.

Table 14-1	Pi Web Servers
Name	**Used For . . .**
apache	Professional web services. Lots of features, can be hard to manage.
nginx	Professional web services. Lots of features, but you can ignore most of them. Easier to set up than Apache.
lighttpd	Very simple web server. Easy to use and set up, but really good only for simple projects. And no one knows how to pronounce the name.
node.js	One of the newest servers. Very flexible, but waaaaaay too complicated for beginners.

Don't try to install more than one server at a time. If you want to experiment with Apache instead of nginx, start with a fresh memory card and a fresh install of Raspbian. Servers don't always play nicely together.

Install nginx

To install nginx:

1. **If you're using the desktop, open a terminal window.**

   If you're not, make sure that you can see the command prompt. (See Chapters 5 and 9 for more about the terminal window and the command line.)

2. **Type the following command and press Enter:**

   ```
   sudo apt-get install nginx
   ```

Figure 14-2 shows what happens next. Your Pi does the usual installation dance. Weird messages that hardly anyone understands scroll by. Eventually the command prompt appears again.

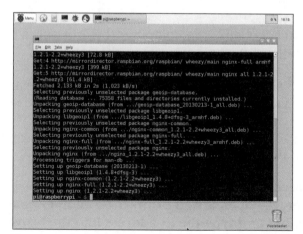

Figure 14-2

Launch nginx

After you install nginx, you have to launch it. The easiest way is to reboot your Pi.

On the desktop, click the Menu button and choose Shutdown. Then click Reboot and OK.

If you're not using the desktop, type the following command and press Enter:

```
sudo reboot
```

Then wait for the usual reboot sequence. At the end of it, log in again and launch the desktop with startx.

This is a rare example of an easy-to-remember Linux command.

Check nginx

To see whether nginx is working, follow these steps:

1. **Open Epiphany on the Pi and type `localhost` into the browser bar.**

   This command checks the computer the browser is running on to see whether it has a web page to show you.

   Figure 14-3 shows you what should happen next — a welcome message that shows nginx is running. It's a genuine web page served by your Pi!

   You're not done yet.

2. **If you already know your Pi's IP address — because you set it in Chapter 5 — open a web browser on another computer on your network and type the IP address into the browser bar.**

3. **If you don't know the address, open a terminal window or use the command prompt and type**

   ```
   hostname -I
   ```

Figure 14-3

4. **Press Enter.**

   You see the IP address.

   If you get the address right, you should be able to see the web page in a browser on any computer, tablet, or smartphone on your network. It just works, and the web page appears as if by magic.

Now you can think about editing the default message so that your page says something more interesting.

 You may be wondering if you can put your Pi's web pages on the Internet. How about giving yourself a mywebsite.com URL? You can, but it's complicated. The next chapter has some notes and hints to get you started. Getting your Pi online is a big, hard project, and for security reasons, it's not a very smart thing to do.

Make Simple Web Pages

The default web page isn't very exciting. But before you change it, you have to work out what to change.

Where do the web files live? Most servers serve files from a standard path. For nginx, that path is

```
/usr/share/nginx/www
```

On the desktop, open the File Manager and work your way to the path, as shown in Figure 14-4. You can see there are a couple of files inside it. Both have the `.html` extension, which tells you they're web content files. They contain the instructions that make a web page appear in your browser.

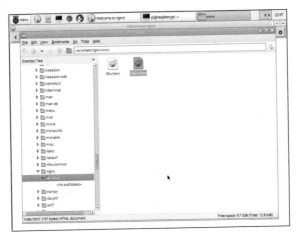

Figure 14-4

HTML stands for Hypertext Markup Language. You don't need to remember what it stands for, but you do need to remember that `.html` files make web pages.

Use index.html

When you ask a web server for a web page, it looks for a file called `index.html`. If it finds the file, the web server sends it to the browser.

To make your page look different, you have to edit this file.

In the File Manager, right-click on `index.html` and choose Text Editor to load the file into the Leaf editor. Figure 14-5 shows the file open for editing.

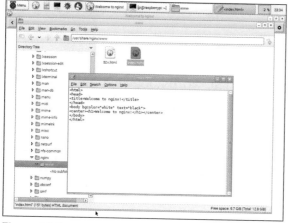

Figure 14-5

What does `50x.html` do? Try looking at `[your pi's IP address]/50x.html` to see. That didn't work, did it? Wait. . . . Yes it did. It's actually an "I couldn't find a file" page. If you give nginx a URL it can't make sense of, it shows the contents of this file. It also shows the contents of the file if you ask for it directly! Usually, files like these are called 404 pages. For some reason, nginx calls its version a 50x page instead.

Understand tags

If you're expecting HTML to look like Python, it doesn't. It looks quirky and strange, `<with><lots><of><angle><brackets>`.

HTML is simpler than it looks. The idea is that you split a page up into sections. You can use ready-made sections for things like page titles and headings. You can also make custom sections of your own.

Sections are marked with *tags,* which are the words that live between <those angle brackets>. Each section has two tags, so the browser knows where it starts and ends. The second tag has an extra backslash to mark the end.

For example,

```
<title>This is the page title</title>
```

makes a title section. The words between the tags are the page title.

 If you're wondering why you can't see the page title in the browser window, it's because the title tags set the text that appears in the browser window's top title bar or in a browser tab. The title text doesn't appear anywhere in the window, which is kind of weird, but huh.

Understand html, head, and body tags

Some of the tags get the browser ready to show the page. They go in a section called the *head.*

The remaining tags include the content that appears on the page. They go in a section called the *body.*

You can also add an html tag. You don't really need it, but it's usually included anyway.

In outline, the tags for a page look like this:

```
<html>
<head>
stuff that sets up the page goes here...
</head>
<body>
stuff you see on the page goes here...
</body>
</html>
```

Grown-up web pages also include something called a *doctype,* which tells the browser how to make sense of the rest of the file. The doctype is a single tag — there's no </doctype> at the end — and it's often followed by technical gibberish. You can ignore doctypes for simple projects.

Fix file permissions

Now you know enough to change the welcome message. You can just edit the text and save it. And you're good to go!

Nope, because permissions. You don't have permission to edit the .html file. It belongs to the root god-user.

Before you can save it, you have to make the welcome message your own. You can do so in various ways. One option is to use a neat feature in File Manager:

1. **Choose Tools ⇨ Open Current Folder in Terminal, as shown in Figure 14-6.**

Figure 14-6

This step does what it says — opens a Terminal window with the path set to the current folder.

Now you can use the Linux chmod and sudo commands to change the permissions on index.html.

2. Type the following code and press Enter:

```
sudo chmod a+w index.html
```

This magic word command makes index.html writeable, so you can change it with the editor and save it.

Change the message

After you change permissions, you can edit the file. Can you guess what you need to change? If you edit the line that says

```
<center><h1>Welcome to nginx!</h1></center>
```

and change the text between the tags, your page will show a different message. Use the Leaf editor to change it to

```
<center><h1>Welcome to my Pi!</h1></center>
```

Choose File ⇨ Save to save the file. Click the reload button in your web browser, and the page shows the new text, as shown in Figure 14-7.

Figure 14-7

Find Out More about Web Design

The page you just made is almost as simple as it gets, but you can make it more interesting.

First, you need to understand what's happening in the other tags:

- The `<body>` tags includes a couple of extra items. The `bgcolor` and `text` items set the page background color and the text color.

- The `<center></center>` tag tells the browser to put the message in the middle of the line.

- The `<h1></h1>` tags tell it to make it a big important page headline. You can make the text smaller by changing `<h1></h1>` to `<h2></h2>` all the way down to `<h5></h5>`, which makes the letters the same size as normal text.

If you want to make simple pages, these tags are almost all you need to know.

Split content and decoration

A basic rule of web design is that you keep content and decoration in separate files.

The `.html` file for a page includes all the words, important photos, web links, YouTube links, and the other content — which means the things that visitors look at and read.

The decoration and styling — colors, page layout, boxes, shapes, letter sizes, letter styles, and even simple animations — live in another file. It has a `.css` extension, and it tells the browser how to make the content look good — or at least, not bad.

Decoration and styling are more of a big deal than maybe they sound. Pages that look good can make the difference between getting a lot of visitors and getting almost none. The styling can also help make a page easier to use.

If this content and decoration split doesn't make sense, take a look at www.csszengarden.com. All the pages on the site have exactly the same content. They all use the same .html file, but they all have different styling, set up in different .css files. The styling makes the pages look completely, amazingly different.

CSS stands for Cascading Style Sheets, which sounds like it should be the name of a Canadian indie band, but isn't. You don't need to remember this abbreviation. You need to remember only that decoration details live inside a .css file.

Get started with CSS

You can make a simple .css file to change the look and the layout of your intro page. You have to do four things:

1. **Create the file.**

2. **Add some decoration commands and save the file.**

3. **Change the .html file to remove all the decoration and styling.**

4. **Change the .html file so it loads the .css file instead.**

The following sections work through each step.

Create a CSS file

To create a CSS file, in the Terminal window for the folder, type these commands and press Enter after each one:

```
sudo touch my.css
sudo chmod a+w my.css
```

You now have an empty file called my.css, and you have the permissions you need to edit it, which is definitely a plus.

If you closed the Terminal window, choose Tool ⇨ Open Current Folder in Terminal to open it. The Linux touch command makes an empty file.

Add decoration

The rule for CSS is that you can add decoration to every tag in your HTML file. Whenever you have a tag like <body> or <h1>, you can set up decoration for it.

Obviously, it would be way too easy if CSS looked like HTML. It doesn't. It looks and works in a completely different way, but it's not hard to use. You just add a tag and put each kind of decoration on a separate line after the tag. Then you wrap all the decoration inside curly brackets. In outline, you get this:

```
tag-name {
decoration statement;
another decoration statement;
keep adding decoration statements until you're done;
}
```

Find out about decoration

How do you know what kind of decoration statements you can use? You look at a CSS reference, like the one at www.w3schools.com/css/default.asp.

There are literally hundreds of decoration options. Most people can't remember all of them. If you want to find out more about CSS, it's a good idea to work through an online tutorial like the one at the link.

There's a lot to learn, but usually you're trying to do basic things like change background colors and letter sizes. You don't need to know much CSS to do those kind of things.

Here's a simple example of CSS styling:

```
body {
background-color: rgb(255, 255, 0);
}
```

```
h1 {
text-align: center;
font-size: 100px;
}
```

In English, the statements means

```
Set the page background color to yellow
Put the main h1 title in the middle of the page
Make it 100 pixels high, which is really big
```

Type the CSS code — not the English! — into your CSS file and save it.

Remove styling from the HTML

Because you've moved the decoration/styling to the CSS file, you need to remove it from the HTML. This means you need to delete the `<center></center>` tags around the `<h1></h1>` line.

You also need to delete everything in the `<body>` opening tag. The `bgcolor` and `text` statements have to go. The contents of the body tag should like this:

```
<body>
<h1>Welcome to my Pi!</h1>
</body>
```

Don't change anything else. Don't delete anything else! Only change what's inside the `<body>` tag. The rest of the file stays as it is.

Load a CSS file into a web page

After you have some CSS, you have to include it in your page. You need to add a magic word line in the head section of the HTML file.

Open the HTML file in the Leaf editor if it isn't already open. Find the `<head>` tag and add this line after it:

```
<link rel = stylesheet type=text/css href=my.css>
```

This line tells the browser to load your CSS file and use the decoration inside it. The last part is the most important. It tells the browser where to find your CSS file and what it's called.

Check the page

To check the page, reload your web page in a browser. You should get something like Figure 14-8. The background is now very yellow. The text is very big. The figure includes the HTML and CSS in separate windows so that you can check that you got them right.

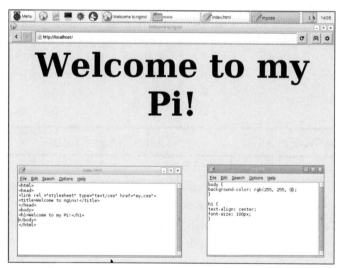

Figure 14-8

You can experiment with making other changes. What happens if you change the rgb values in the background-color statement? What happens if you change the text size to 1000px or 1px?

Play with the CSS statements and see what they do. For extra credit, do some research and add some new statements you haven't used yet.

Go Deeper into CSS and HTML

Skip this section if your brain is overheating and you need a break. You can come back to it later.

Books that tell you all about CSS and HTML are big, thick, and expensive because there's so much to know. But you can make cool pages with only a few more details about things like links, pictures, and other cool stuff.

Use some useful tags

Table 14-2 has a list of more tags you can use. For example, if you want to include a link to Google, the HTML looks like this:

```
<a href = http://www.google.com>This is a link to Google. Why not
           click me?</a>
```

Table 14-2	HTML Cheat Sheet
Tag	Used For . . .
<p></p>	Paragraph text. Use it for large blocks of words on a page. Adds a space between the blocks.
<a href = URL>label</a>	Making web links. Replace URL with the web link in full. Only the label text appears on the page.
<img src = URL></img>	Including a picture or photo from a URL.
 	Splits text onto a new line. Doesn't need a matching </br>.

Table 14-3 has a list of special characters. You can't just type these characters into text because they won't show up on the page. To make them appear, you have to use these special codes with a & at the start and a ; at the end.

Table 14-3	A Few HTML Special Characters
Tag	**Used For . . .**
	Space
&copy;	Copyright symbol: ©
&deg;	Degree symbol: °
&lt;	Left angle bracket: <
&rt;	Right angle bracket: >

The space character is very useful because HTML eats spaces. If you try to show text with a lot of spaces, it only ever shows one space. (Really. This is what it does.) To put the spaces back, repeat   as many times as you need.

Using <div> and custom classes

HTML has only so many ready-made tags. You can run out of them very quickly.

Luckily, you can make your own tags. You can use the <div> tag and include a *class* — which is nothing like a class in school. Here it means a group of things that can share a CSS style.

In an HTML file, a div class looks like this:

```
<div class=my-text>It's awesome!</div>
```

In a CSS file, it looks like this:

```
.my-text {
text-align: center;
font-size: 25px;
}
```

See that period at the start of `.my-text`? It's small, but really important. It's how the CSS file knows you're adding decoration to a class.

You can name your class however you want. The name has to start with a period and a letter, and it can't include spaces. Otherwise, anything works.

Figure 14-9 shows a new version of the page with a div class decorating some new text. Just for fun, the background color is raspberry.

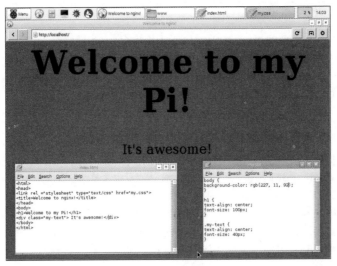

Figure 14-9

If you want to do clever things with page layout, research the CSS box model. You can use CSS layout statements to park your text and pictures anywhere on the screen. There isn't room to explain the box model here. It's complicated, and it has a lot of gotchas that don't quite work how you expect. But if you want to take CSS to the next level, it's the next thing to explore.

Make a Smart Website

# CHAPTER 15

Dumb websites don't change. You get the same content every time you look at them. But a web server is a computer, so you should be able to program it to make a website using code. The code can change the site and make it different every time someone looks at it, or it can make a site that answers questions or allows the user to choose what they see.

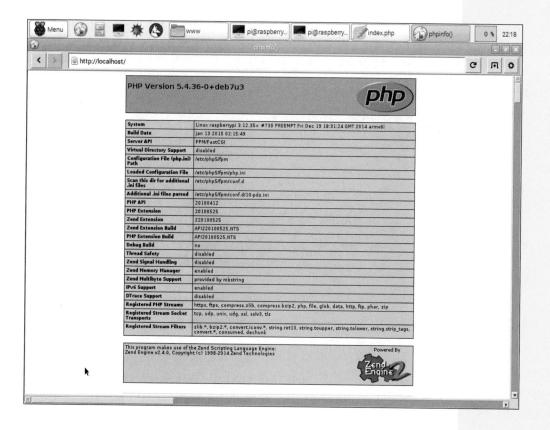

Understand Smart Websites

Most websites are smart. Facebook, Amazon, Google, Yahoo!, and other big names all have very smart sites. When you view a page on these sites, the web server doesn't just spit out a page of canned HTML and CSS.

It builds the page from scratch! In fact, it digs into a library of posts, listings, search results, and all kinds of other information. Then it pulls what it needs from the library, mixes it with some HTML and CSS to lay it out and decorate it, and makes a page for you.

Figure 15-1 shows you what you get on one page on eBay. eBay's web server has built all the photos, menus, links, search boxes, headings, and other text into a page. It does this for every page you look at.

Figure 15-1

Even simple blog sites are smart. You can search the posts, select posts from a month or year, search for topics, and so on.

Making a big smart site is a lot of work for a lot of people, but you can use some of the same tools they use to make a very simple smart site on your Pi. The smart site won't be as complicated as Amazon or eBay, but it will get you started with smart site design.

Meet PHP

You can make a smart website using many different tools. A popular option is a web programming language called PHP. You can write PHP code directly into a file that also includes HTML.

In outline, you use PHP when you want the web server to create some of the content for you. So instead of a fixed message like "My Pi is awesome!", you can use PHP as a fill-in-the-blanks machine that creates a web page that says and does whatever you want.

What do you fill the blanks with? That's up to you! You're limited by your imagination and how much time you want to spend making a site.

Even better, PHP can run other code. You can use it to run Linux commands or Python programs. The possibilities are almost endless.

PHP is short for PHP: Hypertext Processor. The name is an example of recursion, which you can find out about in Chapter 12.

Install PHP

The nginx web server (see Chapter 14) can work with PHP, but it doesn't install it for you. You have to install PHP and set it up before you can use it:

1. **If you're on the desktop, open a terminal window so that you can use the command line.**

2. **Type the following command:**

```
sudo apt-get install php5-fpm
```

3. **Press Enter.**

4. **Press Y and Enter again when asked.**

As usual, a lot of text scrolls by. After a while you'll see the command prompt again.

Set up index.php

PHP doesn't just work. You have to edit a file by hand to tell nginx that you want to use PHP:

1. **Open File Manager and type the following path into the navigation box:**

```
/etc/nginx/sites-available
```

You'll see a file called `default`. You can't edit it because of permissions.

2. **Open a terminal window and type the following, followed by Enter:**

```
sudo chmod a+w default
```

3. **Double-click the file to open it in the Leaf editor.**

You see a file full of what looks like gibberish. The gibberish is a list of settings for nginx. You can ignore most of what you see, but to get PHP working, you have to make some changes.

4. **Scroll down until you see the section that starts with `server` { and look for this line:**

```
index index.html index.htm;
```

5. **Change the line to**

```
index index.php index.html index.htm;
```

This line tells nginx to look for a file called `index.php` instead of a file called `index.html`. If it can't find `index.php`, then it looks for `index.html` instead.

Figure 15-2 shows the file with the line highlighted so that you can see where you need to edit it. (It isn't highlighted in the file. That's just for show.)

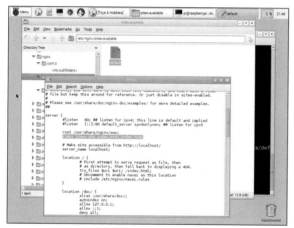

Figure 15-2

As you can maybe guess, you put your PHP code into `index.php`.

Tell nginx to use PHP

To tell nginx to use PHP, scroll down again until you see this line:

```
#location ~ \.php$ {
```

The # signs are like switches. When you include a # sign in the settings, nginx ignores everything on the line after it.

To make PHP work, you have to remove some of the # signs. Look for the following lines and delete the # at the start of each one. Don't change any of the other lines.

```
location ~ \.php$ {
fastcgi_split_path_info ^(.+\.php)(/.+)$;
fastcgi_pass unix:/var/run/php5-fpm.sock;
fastcgi_index index.php;
include fastcgi_params;
}
```

Don't forget the last # in front of the curly bracket! The edited section should look like this:

```
location ~ \.php$ {
        fastcgi_split_path_info ^(.+\.php)(/.+)$;
#       # NOTE: You should have cgi.fix_pathinfo = 0; in php.ini
#
#       # With php5-cgi alone:
#       fastcgi_pass 127.0.0.1:9000;
#       # With php5-fpm:
        fastcgi_pass unix:/var/run/php5-fpm.sock;
            fastcgi_index index.php;
             include fastcgi_params;
}
```

Figure 15-3 has another view.

Reboot

The easiest way to get nginx to use the new settings is to reboot. On the desktop, click the Menu button and choose Shutdown. Then click Reboot and OK.

If you're not using the desktop, type the following command and press Enter:

```
sudo reboot
```

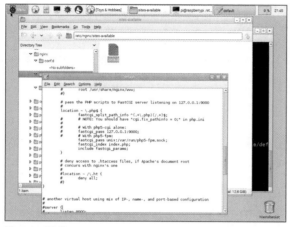

Figure 15-3

Then wait for the usual reboot sequence. At the end of it, log in again and launch the desktop with startx.

Get Started with PHP

If you've just worked through Chapter 14 and you try to load a web page by typing localhost into Epiphany or your Pi's IP address into a browser on another computer, you'll see nginx is still displaying the index.html file.

If you haven't worked through Chapter 14 yet, do it now because you'll need to work with some of the same files and set up the web server and do all kinds of basic stuff like that first.

You haven't made an index.php file yet, but you're about to change that.

To make a file called index.php, follow these steps:

1. **In the File Manager, type the following into the path bar and press Enter:**

   /usr/share/nginx/www

2. **Choose Tools⇨Open Current Folder in Terminal to open a terminal window.**

3. **Type the following commands and press Enter after each one:**

```
sudo touch index.php
sudo chmod a+w index.php
```

This step makes a new file called `index.php` and sets the permissions so that you can edit it in Leaf.

If you're used to working on a PC or a Mac, switching to and from the command line to make files is going to seem like a lot of extra work. And you know what? It absolutely is. If you use Linux a lot, you can make little scripts and shortcuts that speed things up, but it's still more complicated than it needs to be. And unfortunately, that's just how it is.

Check PHP

If you reload your web page, you should see that it's blank. `index.php` has nothing in it. The browser is fine with this — it just displays a blank page.

To make PHP show some content:

1. Open `index.php` in Leaf and add the following line:

```
<?php phpinfo(); ?>
```

Make sure you include all the brackets, question marks, and spaces! If you get anything wrong, the code won't work.

2. **Reload the page again.**

Figure 15-4 shows what you get. Whoa! Where did all that come from? And from just one line! What does it all mean?

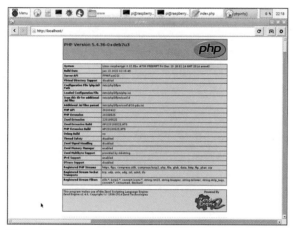

Figure 15-4

You have just made your first smart website.

The one line of code works like this:

```
<?php       # This page is about to run some PHP code
phpinfo();# Make a page that tells me all about PHP
    #on this computer
?>          # We're done with the PHP code.
```

In computertalk, `phpinfo()` is a built-in function. It's a magic word that's part of PHP. If you're a developer, the pages of information it produces tell you which features you can and can't use in your PHP code.

 By way of example, the EXIF section tells you which features are included for reading camera, location, and date/time information out of photos. The openssl section includes information about security. (In fact, it tells you that the security code is out of date.) The details are very technical and only interesting to experts.

If you're not a developer, you can ignore it all. The main thing here is that if you see this page, PHP is working, and you can start using it for cool and useful things.

The other main thing is that PHP is made of built-in functions. They don't all make huge web pages. Most of them do much simpler things. But when you write PHP code, you use the built-in functions and surround them with your own code for doing useful stuff with math and text (strings).

If you want a complete heads-up beginner guide to PHP, visit www.w3schools.com/php/. There is, of course, a lot to learn, but the guide there takes you through it step by step and you can play with the code in your browser, which is cool.

Play with PHP

In this section, you can do something much simpler. You can make PHP show the current date and time. PHP has a built-in function for this task.

Make and display variables

In PHP, variables start with the dollar ($) character, like this:

```
$avariable
```

To make a variable for today's day and date, edit your file so that the code looks like this:

```
<?php
$today=Sunday;
echo $today;
?>
```

PHP code can include all the usual tags you use to build an HTML page. When you ask PHP to display something on a page, you often wrap it in a `div` or some other standard tag. Then you write some CSS to style it. This chapter skips those steps to save space.

If you don't know what CSS and HTML are, read Chapter 14 now.

Here's a cool thing: PHP can also insert tags into a web page, and it can put content between them. *And* it can add CSS to decorate them.

In trained hands, PHP is a total robot web machine.

The `echo` command shows what's inside a variable. It inserts the contents of the variable into the web page so that it appears on the screen when you load the page.

Can you guess what this code does? Save the file and reload the page. You should see Sunday appear.

That's not very exciting — especially if it isn't Sunday. How do you get PHP to show the right day?

Dates and times are often useful, so there's a built-in function you can use. It's called `date()`, which is a total surprise.

Dates are simple. Right?

Not so much. Dates and times are complicated, especially in computers. How do you want the date to appear? Do you want dates in the English/European order (day.month.year) or the US order (month.day.year)? Do you want the full day of the week, or a short version, or no mention of the day at all? Do you want the time, too?

See? Not simple.

Show the date and time

`date()` can handle all the options you can think of and plenty of others, too, but you have to tell it what you want. You tell it what you want by including a *format string,* which is a fancy way of saying that you give it a list of letters, and each letter shows a different part of the date in a different format.

To find out what each letter does, you look up the `date()` page in the PHP manual. Figure 15-5 shows the manual page. You can find it at `http://php.net/manual/en/function.date.php`.

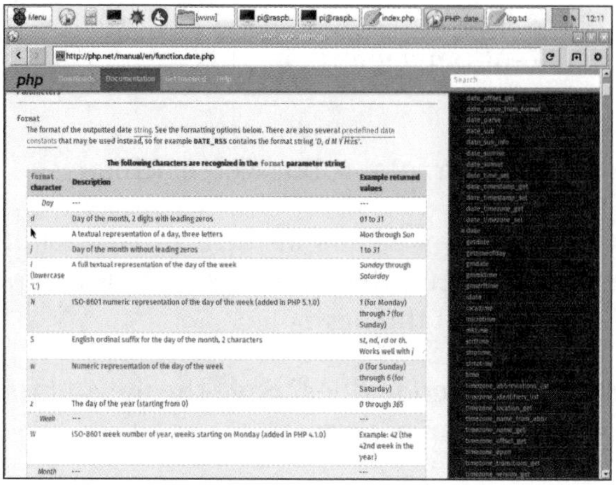

Figure 15-5

Load the page, and you see a lot of letters and options. You probably won't understand most of them, which is totally fine, because
you want your page to do something simple, and you don't care
about making your brain a lot bigger right now. (Isn't it lunch-
time yet?)

To save brain pain, here's a simple example:

```php
<?php
$today = date(F d Y);
echo $today;
?>
```

What does this do? Look up F in the manual. You can maybe
guess from the examples next to the explanation that it means
"Show the name of the month as a word."

How about d? Find it in the manual, read the text, and check
the examples. Show the day of the month as a number. If it's
less than 10, it gets a 0 in front.

And now Y? Show the year as a four-digit number.

You can maybe start to see how this works now. You can add the
time, too. Try it on your own first.

Here's one possible answer:

```
<?php
$today = date(F d Y, g:i:s a);
echo $today;
?>
```

Go through the manual and find out what each letter does. Then see whether you can guess what happens when you put them all together.

See PHP smartness

You should get something like this:

```
March 13 2015, 12:21:53 am
```

And now some magic happens!

The date and time change every time you load the page. You've made a very simple smart web page that updates itself automatically.

You don't have to set the date or time to use this function. The web page is smart enough to show the right date and time whenever you load it.

It works for anyone who visits the site.

Record the date and time

Showing the date and time is a start, but it's not going to set the world on fire. Most people already know the date, and people who are awake sometimes know the time, too.

But PHP isn't just about adding a few simple extras to a page. It's all about making a web server work hard for you. This means you can add kinds of things to all kinds of information: dates, times, names, addresses, phone numbers, email address, Twitter accounts, weather images, news reports, and even information pulled from other web pages.

Pulling information from other web pages and using it on your own page is called *web scraping*. As a topic, web scraping a little too big and complicated for this book, but you can find out more by searching for it online. Python and PHP have ready-made sample code for web scraping, so you don't have to start from scratch to make it work.

Make a file

You can make a slightly more complicated project that remembers the date and time anyone looks at this page. This is often called a *log*.

Computers keep logs because ships used to keep a log book. Ship captains used to work out how fast they were going by throwing a log on the end of a chain overboard and timing how long it took to run out of chain. The measurements were written in a special book. It's a bad idea to measure anything by throwing a computer at it, but log still gets used today.

You need to make a file for your log using a Terminal window. Make sure that you're in the /use/share/nginx/www folder. Then type the following commands and press Enter after each one:

```
sudo touch log.txt
sudo chmod a+w log.txt
```

These commands make an empty log file. Now you can start filling it with dates and times.

It's possible to tell PHP to make a file for you. But the code is a little complicated, and dealing with permissions in PHP makes it even harder.

Tell PHP which file to write to

It's useful to put the path of the log file into a variable. You don't have to do it, but it makes the code slightly easier to read. Putting the path of the log file into a variable also makes it easier to handle more than one log file, if you decide to do that later.

Add this line to your `index.php` file, after the `<?php` line at the start:

```
$log_file = /usr/share/nginx/www/log.txt;
```

This line makes a variable called `log_file` and puts the path you want into it.

Make PHP write the date/time

Saving and loading information can get quite complicated in PHP, but PHP has a neat way to make it simpler. You can use a function called `file_put_contents()` to write some information to a file.

The magic words are here:

```
file_put_contents($log_file, $today, FILE_APPEND);
```

Add them just before the final `?>` in the file. Can you work out what the code does? It writes `$today` to the file you named in `$log_file`. The `FILE_APPEND` line means the new information gets added to the end of the file. Capital letters matter here. You have to type `FILE_APPEND`. Small letters — `file_append` — won't work.

 If you leave out `FILE_APPEND`, the file keeps only the last time/date because it overwrites whatever was already in the file. Sometimes you want this — but not here.

Split up lines

If you save the file now and reload the page a few times, you'll see that `log.txt` starts filling up — but not in a useful way. When you write the date and time to disk, it appears as one long line.

To fix this issue, you have to tell PHP to write each date on a new line. But how do you do that?

As usual, there's a magic word answer — more like a magic letter — so you won't be able to guess the answer unless someone tells you.

PHP and other computer languages use a special trick for putting text on a new line. You have to write a special character called — wait for it . . . a newline.

You won't find the newline on your computer keyboard. It's an example of an *escape code* character.

To make an escape code character, you type a backslash \ to tell PHP that you're doing something special. Then, to make a newline, you follow it with n for newline.

See how the escape code characters work? You can use other escape characters, but for most computer projects only newlines are useful.

To join your newline to existing text, you put a period in front of it. The period character tells PHP to join text strings together.

To make that change, find the line that says

```
$today = date(F d Y, g:i:s a);
```

and change it to

```
$today = date(F d Y, g:i:s a).\n;
```

Now $today works the same way as before, but it includes a newline at the end. So when you add it to the log file, the dates all go on different lines.

Make sure that you type the backslash (\) and not the forward slash (/). The backslash key is near the bottom left of your computer keyboard.

Figure 15-6 puts it all together. You can see the web page displaying the current date and time, the finished `index.php` file, and a
sample log file, which shows a list of the dates and times the page
was viewed.

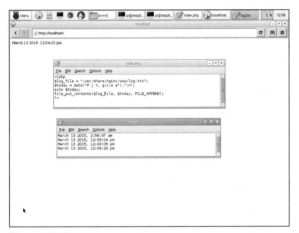

Figure 15-6

Whenever someone visits the page, the date and time get added
to the end, automatically.

Link PHP to Linux

You can find out a lot more about PHP. You can build giant, complicated web machines in PHP. The popular WordPress blogging
system is written in PHP.

This project is just a taster, and there isn't space here to go into
more details. But there is one more very useful feature you should
know about. You can use it to run other software inside PHP code.

PHP has a special function called `shell_exec()`, which is a lot
like having the Linux command line inside a web page.

So you can run any Linux command inside PHP. Here's a simple example. Edit index.php so it looks like this:

```
<?php
$result = shell_exec(ls -Al);
echo <pre>$result</pre>;
?>
```

This code runs the Linux ls command with Al switches to list the contents of the current folder.

What does the <pre></pre> do? If you don't include the tags, you see only the last line of output, which is kind of dumb.

When you run a command, PHP and the web browser add extra formatting, which gets rid of newlines and other characters they think you don't want.

<pre></pre> is a special HTML tag that keeps that from happening. When you use it, the browser shows the output without trying to do anything clever to it. It also uses a letter style that keeps it looking neater than normal web text.

Figure 15-7 shows how the file list appears inside the web page. When you reload the page, it appears in your browser.

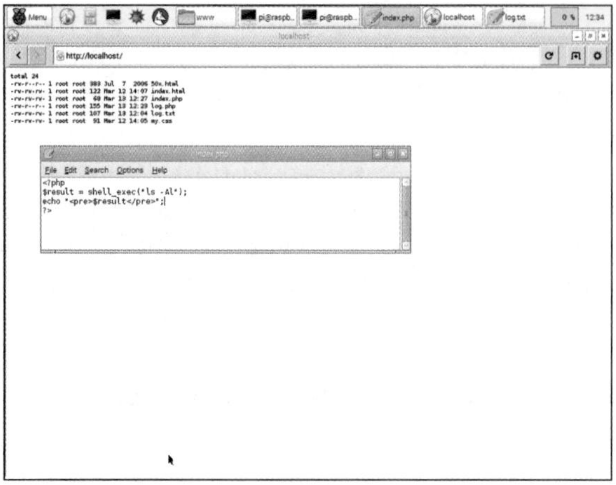

Figure 15-7

Deal with permissions

shell_exec() is great, but there are a few gotchas. When you run a command like ls, it lists the files in the web directory because the command is actually run by the web server.

How does this affect permissions? It can take a while to work out what's happening.

When you use your Pi, you log in as a user called pi. The Pi user does not have god-mode privileges, so you have to do all that stuff with the sudo command (see Chapter 11) to do god-mode things.

The nginx web server runs as a user, too. The user is called www-data but doesn't have god-mode privileges either.

But you can use sudo, right? Nope. For security reasons, shell_exec() doesn't let you use sudo. If you try to run a sudo command, shell_exec() does nothing at all.

So you can't do as much with shell_exec() as you'd like to. You can do almost anything you can do as a normal user, but you can't do anything that needs god-mode.

Permission issues aren't always a problem. If you need to read or write some files you can't usually access, you can use chmod to set their permissions before you try to access them from PHP.

But there's no getting around that it's extra work, it's easy to forget to do it, and generally it's not as fun as it could be.

Use Python in PHP

Here's one more trick — running Python from PHP.

To run Python from PHP:

1. **Open a terminal window and type the following commands, pressing Enter after each one:**

   ```
   sudo touch simple.py
   sudo chmod a+wx simple.py
   ```

Don't miss the extra x in the `chmod` command. You have to set up the Python file so that it can be executed — run as a program. That's what the extra x is for. The w makes it editable, as usual.

2. **Open `simple.py` in Leaf and add one line of code:**

```
print Hello, Python!
```

3. **Save and close the file.**

4. **Now change `index.php` so it looks like this:**

```php
<?php
$result = shell_exec(python simple.py);
echo <pre>$result</pre>;
?>
```

5. **Save the file and reload the page.**

You should get Figure 15-8. (The output text may be too small to read, but it really does say, "Hello, Python!")

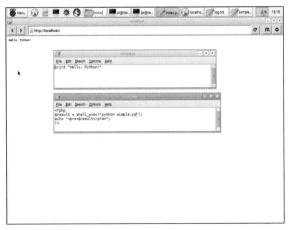

Figure 15-8

`simple.py` is a very, very simple Python program. Of course, the Python code can be as complicated as you want it to be. Any text it creates gets piped straight through to the web page, so you can use Python to make almost any kind of web content you want.

One thing you can't do is make turtle graphics. Your Python code can send text only to the web page, not pictures. There are ways to change this, but they're complicated. In outline, you save the pictures to an image file, convert the image file into a different kind of image file, and then load that image into your page. If you want a challenge, see whether you can make that happen. It's really not easy at all, but it's very satisfying if you can make it work.

Put it all together

As with PHP, you can embed the output of Python code inside static HTML tags. Or you can use the code to build tags into the output so that the formatting and styling of your page are made by code instead of made by hand. (Want to try it? Get rid of the `<pre></pre>` tags. Otherwise, the code won't work.)

Although this project has only very simple examples, you can maybe understand just how much you can do with smart server code. You now know enough to start thinking about building entire web pages using code. Making something big and complicated will take a while, but if you break it down into small sections it's not any harder than any other kind of coding.

A Quick Note about JavaScript

Part IV introduces Linux, Python, HTML, CSS, PHP. Would you believe there's yet another programming language you can learn?

It's called JavaScript, and it's often used inside web pages. Unlike Python and the rest, it's *event-driven,* which means it doesn't start at the beginning of a file and work its way to the end, in order.

Instead, it's more like a collection of mini-programs that run whenever a user does something:

✔ When she opens the web page, some code runs.

✔ When she clicks the mouse, other code runs.

✔ When she scrolls the page, still other code runs.

✔ When she moves the mouse over a button or menu, yep, more code runs.

This book doesn't have the space to introduce you to JavaScript as well. It's more complicated than PHP or Python because it's hooked very deeply into the plumbing that runs behind the scenes of a web page.

If you want an introduction, see the tutorial at www.w3schools. com/js in Figure 15-9.

Figure 15-9

There's a lot to learn, so you'll likely want to spend more time with Python and PHP first. But if you're thinking that maybe you want to know more about web design, JavaScript is a good next step.

Week 5
Working with a Webcam

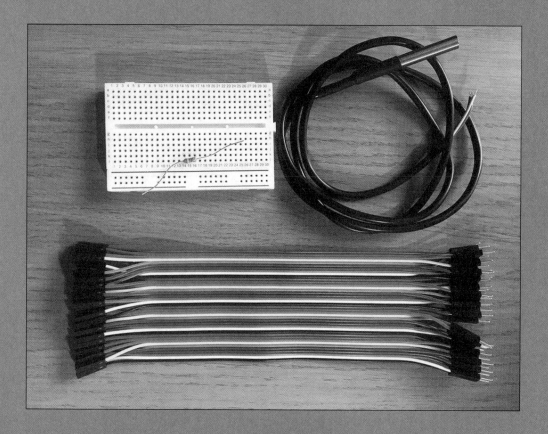

In this part, you'll . . .

Take Photos with a Webcam

Wouldn't it be cool to turn your Pi into a camera? It's not hard, and you can use a cheap webcam as your camera.

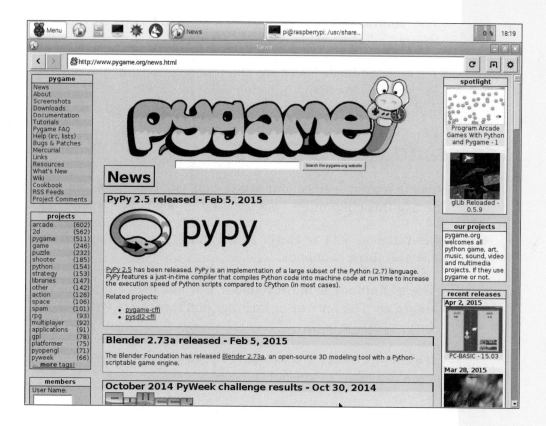

Understand Webcams

Why can't you make a streaming video cam? Streaming webcams look simple, but they aren't. The technology and the code used to make them work are complicated. The basic problems are

- **The technology is flaky.** Some webcams can do it. Others can't. You can't be sure whether your webcam works until you try it.

- **It's complicated.** You have to do a lot of installing and setting up, and a lot can go wrong.

- **It's nonstandard.** There are different solutions for the official Pi camera add-on and for other webcams.

Understand Photo Cams

Instead of making a streaming video cam, you can make a photo camera in this chapter and put it on a web page in Chapter 17.

A photo camera isn't as clever as streaming video to the web, but it solves all three problems:

- **The technology is more reliable.** It works with almost all webcams. The only webcams that don't work are very old, very cheap, or both.

- **It's simple.** It uses Python and PHP, so you don't need to install any new or special software.

- **It's standard.** You have to type an extra one-line command to get the official add-on Pi camera to work with it. Otherwise, all cameras work with the same code.

Choose a Webcam

Many people have a spare webcam. Perhaps it's used for Skype or Facetime or some other video chat system.

If you don't already have a webcam, you can buy one online from Amazon or from almost any large supermarket. Figure 16-1 shows some of the many webcams available.

Figure 16-1

Some cost more than $100. But you don't need a super-expensive webcam for this project. Any model costing more than $20 should work fine.

The code was tested with a Logitech C270HD webcam, which costs less than $25 in the United States and around £15 in the UK.

To set up the webcam, plug it into a USB port. If you're using a hub, plug it into the hub. Linux includes basic drivers, so it should just work.

Use the RPI Camera

If you have an official RPI Camera instead of a webcam, you have to type a special magic word command to use it for this project:

```
sudo modprobe bcm2835-v4l2
```

Make sure that you get all the numbers and letters right! You have to type this command whenever you reboot your Pi. Otherwise, your RPI camera won't work.

Don't type the command if you're using a USB webcam. You don't need it!

To save retyping it, you can add the command to a file called `/etc/rc.local`, which is used for commands that run when the Pi boots. You have to promote yourself to root to edit this file.

Meet Pygame

Loading a photo from a webcam is hard. If you had to write all the code yourself, it would take you a very long time, and it probably wouldn't work with more than a few webcams — because they're all slightly different.

Luckily, there's a simple way to fix this problem.

Python includes an optional module called Pygame. The official website at `http://pygame.org` is shown in Figure 16-2.

Figure 16-2

Pygame was designed for game coding. It can draw blocks in a window, move sprites around, check if they're touching, and so on. It's like a grown-up version of Scratch, built into Python.

If you were using the rest of Pygame, you would add `pygame.init()`, too. You're not, so you don't need to.

For this project, you can ignore the game features. You don't need to use sprites or draw boxes.

What's relevant to your interests here is the fact that Pygame has a simple photo grabber. It works with most webcams, and you can plug it into any Python project with only a few lines of code.

The grabber isn't fast. It takes a couple of seconds to take a photo and save it, so there's no way to get video out of it. But it's easy to use, and it doesn't need any driver software or other add-ons.

Pygame is a good way to find out more about Python. It's not fast enough or clever enough to make commercial games you can sell, but it's an excellent way to start learning about hands-on Python techniques. You can explore thousands of examples on the Pygame website.

Add Pygame to a Python project

Pygame is built into Python. It's one of the many modules — add-ons — included in Python. You don't have to install it separately, but you do need to tell Python you want to use it. The official way to tell Python you want to use a module is the import command, followed by the module name:

```
import pygame
```

Sometimes you also need to import specific features from the module. Here you need the camera, so you need to add

```
import pygame.camera
```

How do you know when you need to import extra features? There's no logic to this — you have to look for examples online and copy them.

Fire up the camera

Many modules have a special setup option. It's often called `init`, which is short for initialization.

Modules are like a kit of parts. There may be tens or hundreds of parts with different names, and they all do something unique and possibly useful.

To use a part, you type the name of the module, a period, and the name of the part. If parts have subparts, you keep going until you're done.

To set up the camera, you have to add these lines:

```
pygame.init()
pygame.camera.init()
```

If you leave out the first line, the code works . . . sometimes. It's best to set up Pygame properly before using it.

Set the width and height

How big do you want your grabs? Pygame gives you a choice. It's limited by the maximum resolution of the webcam, but you can experiment with different settings to trade off quality against speed — it takes longer to capture a photo with a higher resolution and more detail.

Because you may want to change the width and the height of the photo and also to make your code easier to read, you can put the width and height into two variables called width and height.

The sample code for this project includes a list of other possible photo sizes. You can use one of the smaller sizes for speed:

```
width = 640
height = 480
```

Set up the webcam for photos

After you set the width and height, you need to make a virtual camera in software. This virtual camera is like a giant variable with super-powers. It's literally the software equivalent of your webcam. Instead of pushing buttons on the webcam case, you send commands to the virtual camera.

Variables with super-powers like this are sometimes called *objects.* They include variables of their own — sometimes lots of variables — and they come with a built-in list of commands.

You send commands to the object to make it do useful stuff. The variables and commands — sometimes called *methods* — for ready-made objects like the Pygame camera are listed in the help documentation.

The Pygame camera does a lot of complicated things and has a lot of complicated settings you don't need to worry about, because the default — start-up — values work fine.

You only need to tell it three things: the width of a grab, the height of a grab, and a file path to the video from the camera.

The width and height are easy. But what about the video? Linux uses a special directory called /dev to handle hardware. If you list the files in /dev with the ls -l command, you see something like Figure 16-3, with a long list of devices.

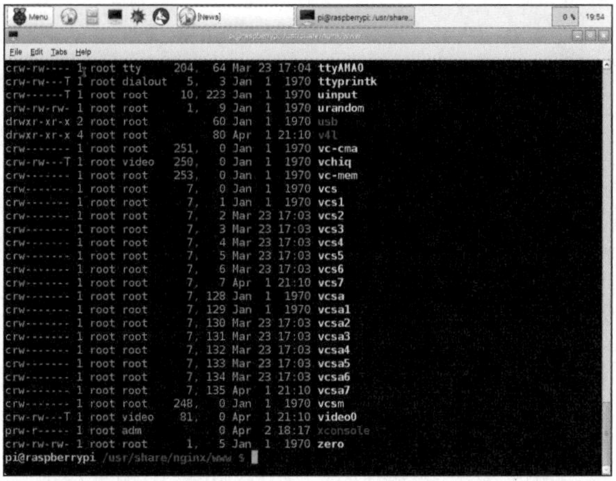

Figure 16-3

One of the devices is video0, so it's a good bet the location of the video source is `/dev/video0`.

The finished setup code looks like this:

```
cam = pygame.camera.Camera(/dev/video0, (width, height))
```

One of the weird, possibly brilliant, things about Linux is that everything is a file, so a video feed is a file, too. It's just a never-ending file you can dip into when you need to. `/dev` files have permission settings just like normal files.

The permissions aren't quite the same as the ones you find on normal files. There's a c at the start of the permissions, which is how Linux tells you the device produces a stream of small numbers — characters. There's also a T at the end, which is a special permission you can apply when you don't want to delete a file. (You don't need to remember these permissions.)

Take and Save a Photo

After the webcam is ready, you can add code to take a photo. The magic word code is

```
cam.start()
image = cam.get_image()
cam.stop()
```

This code tells the camera object you made to get ready for a photo. Then it tells it to take a photo. Then it tells it to go back to waiting patiently while you do other stuff, like looking at the photo and saying "Ooooh!"

That's all the code you need. Pygame handles the rest.

Pygame also handles image saving, with one more line:

```
pygame.image.save(image, 'cam.jpg')
```

See how useful Pygame is? You don't have to worry about converting the file to numbers or anything complicated like that. Pygame does it all for you.

Putting it all together, the code looks like this:

```
import pygame
import pygame.camera
pygame.init()
pygame.camera.init()
width = 640
height = 480
cam = pygame.camera.Camera(/dev/video0, (width, height))
cam.start()
image = cam.get_image()
cam.stop()
pygame.image.save(image, 'cam.jpg')
```

Run and check the code

To test the code, make a new file in your `pi` directory with either the touch command or the Leaf editor. Type the code. Save it as `webcam.py`.

If you're feeling lazy — you are, aren't you? — you can download the code from the book's website at `www.dummies.com/extras/raspberrypiforkids`.

To check the code, make sure that you're in your `pi` directory so that Python can find the file. Then type the following command and press Enter:

```
python webcam.py
```

If you typed the code with no mistakes and you're in the right directory, you should see no error messages.

Figure 16-4 demonstrates what happens when you list the directory, run the code, and then list the directory again.

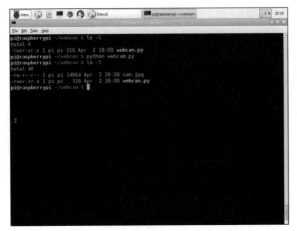

Figure 16-4

A new file appears! It's called cam.jpg.

 In this example, the code and image went into a special directory called webcam. It's often good to keep projects in separate folders. The folder has nothing else in it. If you made your files in /home/pi, you see other stuff in there, too, when you look.

Look at the photo

To view the photo, open File Manager on the desktop and navigate to the directory with your script. If you haven't changed File Manager's settings, you can see your script and a preview of the cam.jpg file.

To view the file full size, double-click it to open the build in image viewer app, as shown in Figure 16-5.

To take a different photo, run the script again.

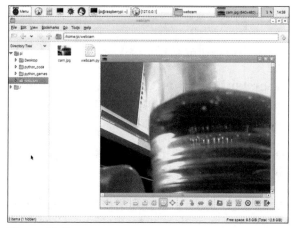

Figure 16-5

Fix Problems

If the code didn't work, try the following:

- **Triple-check for typos.** Did you leave out any letters? Did you add something by accident? Did you get the order of the lines right? Did you add or remove a bracket?

- **Check whether you're in the right directory.** You should be in /home/pi or a directory inside /home/pi. If you're not, you may get permission problems.

- **Is the webcam connected to your Pi?** Always worth checking . . .

- **Does the webcam work?** If not, try a different, more expensive webcam.

Improve the Script

There are a few obvious things you can do to improve the code:

- ✔ **Save the image with the time and date in the filename.** Chapter 15 has some hints about working with times and dates.

- ✔ **Use `pygame.transform()` commands to flip, turn, or resize the photo before you save it.**

- ✔ **Add Instagram-style blur and color effects to the photo before saving it.** This option is really hard. Don't worry if you can't do it — you have to research a *lot* about Python and images to make it work.

- ✔ **Work out how to make your code use switches so that you can set the photo size from the command line when you run the script.** This one is hard, too. The magic words to search for online are Python command-line arguments.

A lot of results mention *parsing,* which is computertalk for reading a list of things and making sense of what we're supposed to do with them. It's like the word "understanding" but for geeks.

Make a Simple Webcam

In Chapter 16, you can make a simple camera. How about putting the photo it takes onto a web page to make a webcam? You can leave the cam in your room to check on pets, brothers, sisters, or other aliens.

Set Up a Webpage

If you read Chapter 15, you know that you can put the Python script inside a PHP script and it should work. Right?

Try it. You can use the PHP file from Chapter 15 or make a new one in the `/usr/share/nginx/www` directory. Make sure that it's called `index.php`.

Instead of using Leaf on the desktop, you can edit the file in a more Linux-y kind of a way.

Meet nano

In Chapter 15, you can find out how use the `touch` and `chmod` commands to make a new file and then make it editable in the Leaf desktop editor.

There's a better way!

Linux includes an editor that works from the command line. It's called `nano`. You can use it with `sudo` to edit any file or make a new file as root.

Compared to a desktop text editor, `nano` can feel strange and even clumsy. But once you get used to it, it's quicker.

Because `nano` works from the command line, you can't use it with a mouse. Instead, you have to type commands. All the commands work the same way: You hold down the Control key, and you type a letter.

You don't press Enter when you're using `nano` commands. Holding down the Control key tells `nano` that you're typing a command and not editing the text.

The full list of commands is long, but you can see a handy summary of the most useful commands at the bottom of the editing window, as shown in Figure 17-1.

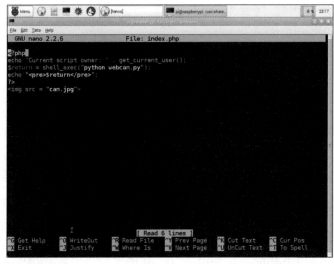

Figure 17-1

You can use the cd command to move to /usr/share/nginx/ www. Then type the following command and press Enter:

```
sudo nano index.php
```

Colors! nano highlights different parts of the code in different colors. Adding color isn't always useful, but it makes it easier to see what the code is doing.

Without a mouse, you have to use the *cursor* — the filled-in rectangle — to keep track of where you are. Use the arrow keys to move the cursor.

To add text, start typing. To delete text, press the Delete key (right delete) or Backspace (left delete.) To add a new line, press Enter.

Table 17-1 lists the most useful nano commands. Unless you're doing something difficult — you aren't here — you can ignore all the others.

Table 17-1	Useful nano Commands
Tag	Used For . . .
Control+Y	Move up a page
Control+V	Move down a page
Control+K	Cut a line to delete it
Control+U	Undelete (paste) a line
Control+O	Save the current file
Control+X	Quit nano
Control+G	List other commands

Write a PHP script

If you read Chapter 15, you have an idea of what should go inside the PHP file. Here's one solution:

```
<?php
$return = shell_exec(python webcam.py);
echo <pre>$return</pre>;
?>
<img src = cam.jpg>
```

The second line runs the script. The last line displays the image on a web page.

Technically, the code doesn't really need the $return variable because the Python code doesn't return anything — it just makes a new file instead. But often it's useful to have the option of a return value in case you decide to use it later — maybe for testing and problem-solving.

Copy and save files

There's an obvious problem: When you run the PHP code, Python looks for the webcam.py file in the nginx www directory, but the file is in your /home/pi directory.

You can tell the script to run the file from the pi directory, but it's better to keep everything in one place.

So you have to copy the script before you can run it, using the cp command, like this:

```
sudo cp /home/pi/webcam.py webcam.py
```

The first path should find the file in your home directory. If you put it in a special project directory, include the full path to the project.

Now you have a copy of the Python file. It's owned by root. What happens if you try to run it?

Check the web page

Open a browser on the Pi or on some other computer on your home network and type the Pi's IP address into the address bar.

If you don't know the IP address, Chapters 14 and 15 tell you how to find it. On the Pi, you can type localhost or 127.0.0.1 instead.

Do you get a photo? Or do you get something like Figure 17-2, with a placeholder for a missing image?

Uh oh. . . .

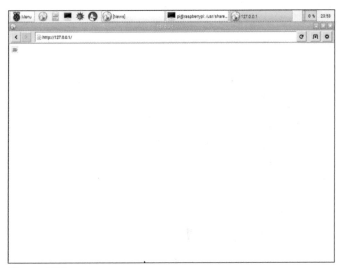

Figure 17-2

Debug a Web Page

When something goes wrong, how can you fix it?

It can be hard, especially when you're working with Python and PHP. Pages often *fail silently.* You literally get no clues — no error messages, no log files you can check, nothing at all.

Think about permissions

If you read Chapters 12 and 13 in this book, you may be wondering if there is a problem with permissions. There is! But to fix it, you have to understand more about nginx.

What happens when the web server runs? You can't fix permissions unless you know who the user is. Which user owns the web server? Is it pi, or root, or some other user?

You can try guessing, but if you don't know the answer, you'll guess wrong!

To see why, make a new file called whoami.php, with the following contents:

```
<?php
$return = shell_exec(whoami);
echo <pre>$return</pre>;
?>
```

The whoami Linux commands tells you the name of the current user. If you run the command as the pi user, of course you get pi.

If you include it in a script you can find the user of the script — and that may not be pi or root either.

Find the web user

If you reload the page, it produces an unexpected name in very tiny letters: www-data.

Huh? Who's `www-data`? Maybe you remember from Chapters 12 and 13 that apps have their own users. Here, `www-data` is the username nginx hides behind when it's serving a web page.

This user needs permissions to do the following:

✔ Read a picture from the webcam

✔ Save a file to `/usr/share/nginx/www`

Fix the video device permissions

You may think that you have to give `www-data` read access to `/dev/video0`, and everything will be fine.

Unfortunately, that's not enough to fix the problem. To see why, type the following (and press Enter afterwards):

```
groups pi
```

Figure 17-3 shows the list of groups the pi user belongs to.

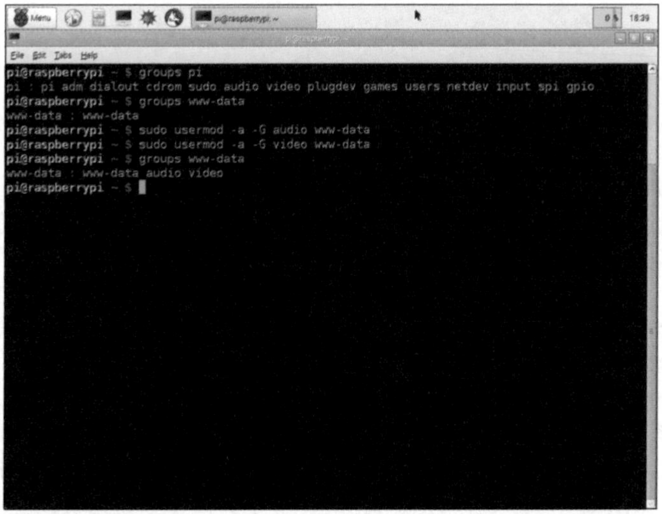

Figure 17-3

Now you have to put on your best detective hat and do some work.

When you made the `webcam.py` script in Chapter 16, it worked fine for the pi user, so you know the pi user is in the right groups to access the webcam.

What happens if you check the groups for `www-data`? Try it with

```
groups www-data
```

`www-data` belongs to its own group, and that's all it belongs to. This means the webcam won't work until you sign up `www-data` to more groups.

It's a good bet that if you're working with video, you need to be a member of the video group, so you have to add `www-data` to the video group before it can use the camera.

And because a webcam has a microphone, you also have to add it to the audio group — even though you're not trying to record audio. Under the hood, Pygame does a blanket gimme everything when it grabs an image.

You have to add `www-data` to the audio group, too, like this:

```
sudo usermod -a -G audio www-data
sudo usermod -a -G video www-data
sudo reboot
```

Rebooting loads the permissions into the rest of Linux and sets them up in the web server. Now your script can access the webcam.

How would you know all this? You wouldn't. You'd use the advanced debugging tricks at the end of this chapter to read some error messages. Then you'd do a lot of web searching and some guessing to try out different things that might work. That's often how it goes with Linux. It's one puzzle after another, until you get some experience. The puzzles *never* go away. You just get better at guessing answers.

Fix web directory permissions

The `www-data` user doesn't have permission to write a file in the `/usr/share/nginx/www` directory.

This limitation is a deliberate security choice to help keep hackers out. Unfortunately, it makes it hard for you to do simple things — for example, saving a web cam image.

The fix is easy. You have to change the owner and the group membership of the `www directory` like this:

```
sudo chgrp www-data /usr/share/nginx/www
sudo chown www-data /usr/share/nginx/www
```

Now `www-data` can make a file in its own directory. Yay!

Figure 17-4 shows the webcam working.

Figure 17-4

Do More Advanced Debugging

Permissions aren't always quite so difficult. After a while, you get used to thinking about groups and directories. For future web projects, you know that the important user is called `www-data` and that you need to reboot to get group and user permissions working.

But Python and PHP can still be awkward. The following sections describe a few tricks you can try when you have a nonworking Python or PHP script and you have no idea what's wrong with it.

Test code with messages

Trick #1 is to put a message into a Python file on a web page and to keep moving it around until you find where the script stops working. The message can be very simple:

```
echo ok
```

The trick works because when PHP runs into a problem with a Python file, it gives up. So you can turn off lines that may be causing problems with a # — which turns them into comments that Python ignores.

Then you can move the test message down line by line until it doesn't appear when you load the page.

Here's an example:

```
cam = pygame.camera.Camera(/dev/video0, (width, height))
echo ok
# cam.start()
# image = cam.get_image()
# cam.stop()
# pygame.image.save(image, 'cam.jpg')
```

If you see an ok, you can try this:

```
cam = pygame.camera.Camera(/dev/video0, (width, height))
cam.start()
echo ok
# image = cam.get_image()
# cam.stop()
# pygame.image.save(image, 'cam.jpg')
```

And then this:

```
cam = pygame.camera.Camera(/dev/video0, (width, height))
cam.start()
image = cam.get_image()
echo ok
# cam.stop()
# pygame.image.save(image, 'cam.jpg')
```

And so on. When the message stops appearing, you've found a line that doesn't work.

Impersonate users

Trick #2: Impersonate www-data. You can use the sudo command to pretend to be the www-data user, like this:

```
sudo — www-data
```

The minus sign is important. It's the world's shortest and least obvious switch.

When you run the command — you have to press Enter after it, as usual — sudo logs you in as www-data. You can cd to /usr/share/nginx/www and run a Python script to see what happens.

This trick is magic because you get to pretend to be a web server. Error messages stop being invisible and start appearing on the screen. You can read them and start guessing how to fix them.

So Python shows you what the problem is — if there is one.

Run PHP from the command line

Trick #3: Running PHP from the command line. You don't have to use PHP inside a web page! You can download an optional add-on to PHP that runs PHP files as a command — and shows you any error messages that appear.

To install this option, type the following and press Enter:

```
sudo apt-get install -y php5-cli
```

Then type the following to see what happens:

```
php index.php
```

Optionally — and usefully — you can try impersonating a user at the same time.

Give up

Trick #4: Give up. Don't give up permanently. But it's fine to give up for a while and come back to a problem later. Sometimes you just need to sleep on a problem, and when you wake up, the answer is obvious!

Index

About the Author

Richard Wentk has been building things out of electronic parts and code for more than 35 years. He is a regular contributor to various UK technology magazines and is the author of *Teach Yourself Visually Raspberry Pi, iOS App Development Portable Genius,* and more than ten other titles. He lives on the South Coast of England surrounded by beaches, gardens, high-speed broadband, and an inexplicably large collection of Raspberry Pis.

Dedication

Dedicated to Team HGA. (*Scientia potestas est.*)

Author's Acknowledgments

Books are always a team effort. I'd like to thank Katie Mohr for getting the project started, Kelly Ewing for shepherding it to a successful conclusion, and Rui Santos for assiduous comments and feedback.

Of course, the book wouldn't have been possible without the efforts of the Raspberry Pi Foundation to bring affordable computing to a new generation and to the thousands of developers who contribute their time and expertise for free in the Open Source community to make projects like the Pi possible. They also deserve many thanks.

Publisher's Acknowledgments

Senior Acquisitions Editor: Katie Mohr

Project Editor: Kelly Ewing

Copy Editor: Kelly Ewing

Editorial Assistant: Claire Brock

Sr. Editorial Assistant: Cherie Case

Production Editor: Suresh Srinivasan

Cover Image: ©Wiley

Apple & Mac

iPad For Dummies,
7th Edition
978-1-118-72306-7

iPhone For Dummies,
7th Edition
978-1-118-69083-3

Macs All-in-One
For Dummies, 4th Edition
978-1-118-82210-4

OS X Mavericks
For Dummies
978-1-118-69188-5

Blogging & Social Media

Facebook For Dummies,
5th Edition
978-1-118-63312-0

Social Media Engagement
For Dummies
978-1-118-53019-1

WordPress For Dummies,
6th Edition
978-1-118-79161-5

Business

Stock Investing
For Dummies, 4th Edition
978-1-118-37678-2

Investing For Dummies,
6th Edition
978-0-470-90545-6

Personal Finance
For Dummies, 7th Edition
978-1-118-11785-9

QuickBooks 2014
For Dummies
978-1-118-72005-9

Small Business Marketing
Kit For Dummies,
3rd Edition
978-1-118-31183-7

Careers

Job Interviews
For Dummies, 4th Edition
978-1-118-11290-8

Job Searching with Social
Media For Dummies,
2nd Edition
978-1-118-67856-5

Personal Branding
For Dummies
978-1-118-11792-7

Resumes For Dummies,
6th Edition
978-0-470-87361-8

Starting an Etsy Business
For Dummies, 2nd Edition
978-1-118-59024-9

Diet & Nutrition

Belly Fat Diet For Dummies
978-1-118-34585-6

Mediterranean Diet
For Dummies
978-1-118-71525-3

Nutrition For Dummies,
5th Edition
978-0-470-93231-5

Digital Photography

Digital SLR Photography
All-in-One For Dummies,
2nd Edition
978-1-118-59082-9

Digital SLR Video &
Filmmaking For Dummies
978-1-118-36598-4

Photoshop Elements 12
For Dummies
978-1-118-72714-0

Gardening

Herb Gardening
For Dummies, 2nd Edition
978-0-470-61778-6

Gardening with Free-Range
Chickens For Dummies
978-1-118-54754-0

Health

Boosting Your Immunity
For Dummies
978-1-118-40200-9

Diabetes For Dummies,
4th Edition
978-1-118-29447-5

Living Paleo For Dummies
978-1-118-29405-5

Big Data

Big Data For Dummies
978-1-118-50422-2

Data Visualization
For Dummies
978-1-118-50289-1

Hadoop For Dummies
978-1-118-60755-8

Language & Foreign Language

500 Spanish Verbs
For Dummies
978-1-118-02382-2

English Grammar
For Dummies, 2nd Edition
978-0-470-54664-2

French All-in-One
For Dummies
978-1-118-22815-9

German Essentials
For Dummies
978-1-118-18422-6

Italian For Dummies,
2nd Edition
978-1-118-00465-4

---

e Available in print and e-book formats.

Available wherever books are sold. **For more information or to order direct visit www.dummies.com**

Math & Science

Algebra I For Dummies,
2nd Edition
978-0-470-55964-2

Anatomy and Physiology
For Dummies, 2nd Edition
978-0-470-92326-9

Astronomy For Dummies,
3rd Edition
978-1-118-37697-3

Biology For Dummies,
2nd Edition
978-0-470-59875-7

Chemistry For Dummies,
2nd Edition
978-1-118-00730-3

1001 Algebra II Practice
Problems For Dummies
978-1-118-44662-1

Microsoft Office

Excel 2013 For Dummies
978-1-118-51012-4

Office 2013 All-in-One
For Dummies
978-1-118-51636-2

PowerPoint 2013
For Dummies
978-1-118-50253-2

Word 2013 For Dummies
978-1-118-49123-2

Music

Blues Harmonica
For Dummies
978-1-118-25269-7

Guitar For Dummies,
3rd Edition
978-1-118-11554-1

iPod & iTunes
For Dummies, 10th Edition
978-1-118-50864-0

Programming

Beginning Programming
with C For Dummies
978-1-118-73763-7

Excel VBA Programming
For Dummies, 3rd Edition
978-1-118-49037-2

Java For Dummies,
6th Edition
978-1-118-40780-6

Religion & Inspiration

The Bible For Dummies
978-0-7645-5296-0

Buddhism For Dummies,
2nd Edition
978-1-118-02379-2

Catholicism For Dummies,
2nd Edition
978-1-118-07778-8

Self-Help & Relationships

Beating Sugar Addiction
For Dummies
978-1-118-54645-1

Meditation For Dummies,
3rd Edition
978-1-118-29144-3

Seniors

Laptops For Seniors
For Dummies, 3rd Edition
978-1-118-71105-7

Computers For Seniors
For Dummies, 3rd Edition
978-1-118-11553-4

iPad For Seniors
For Dummies, 6th Edition
978-1-118-72826-0

Social Security
For Dummies
978-1-118-20573-0

Smartphones & Tablets

Android Phones
For Dummies, 2nd Edition
978-1-118-72030-1

Nexus Tablets
For Dummies
978-1-118-77243-0

Samsung Galaxy S 4
For Dummies
978-1-118-64222-1

Samsung Galaxy Tabs
For Dummies
978-1-118-77294-2

Test Prep

ACT For Dummies,
5th Edition
978-1-118-01259-8

ASVAB For Dummies,
3rd Edition
978-0-470-63760-9

GRE For Dummies,
7th Edition
978-0-470-88921-3

Officer Candidate Tests
For Dummies
978-0-470-59876-4

Physician's Assistant Exam
For Dummies
978-1-118-11556-5

Series 7 Exam For Dummies
978-0-470-09932-2

Windows 8

Windows 8.1 All-in-One
For Dummies
978-1-118-82087-2

Windows 8.1 For Dummies
978-1-118-82121-3

Windows 8.1 For Dummies
Book + DVD Bundle
978-1-118-82107-7

Ⓔ Available in print and e-book formats.

Available wherever books are sold. For more information or to order direct visit www.dummies.com